1001 WAYS
TO MAKE
MONEY
IF YOU DARE

1001 WAYS TO MAKE MONEY IF YOU DARE

TRENT HAMM, AUTHOR OF *365 WAYS TO LIVE CHEAP*

AVON, MASSACHUSETTS

Published by Adams Business, an imprint of Adams Media, a division of F+W Media, Inc.
57 Littlefield Street, Avon, MA 02322. U.S.A.
www.adamsmedia.com

ISBN 10: 1-59869-885-0
ISBN 13: 978-1-59869-885-5

Printed in the United States of America.

J I H G F E D C B A

Library of Congress Cataloging-in-Publication Data
is available from the publisher.

This publication is designed to provide accurate and authoritative information with regard to the subject matter covered. It is sold with the understanding that the publisher is not engaged in rendering legal, accounting, or other professional advice. If legal advice or other expert assistance is required, the services of a competent professional person should be sought.

—From a *Declaration of Principles* jointly adopted by a Committee of the American Bar Association and a Committee of Publishers and Associations

Many of the designations used by manufacturers and sellers to distinguish their product are claimed as trademarks. Where those designations appear in this book and Adams Media was aware of a trademark claim, the designations have been printed with initial capital letters.

Due to the potential for hazard, every precaution should be taken before attempting any actions listed in this book. The author, Adams Media, and F+W Media, Inc. do not accept liability for any injury, loss, or incidental or consequential damage incurred by reliance on the information or advice provided in this book.

Interior illustrations © comstock.com

This book is available at quantity discounts for bulk purchases. For information, please call 1-800-289-0963

Contents

Disclaimer: Please Read—*For Real*

Just in case you missed the title of this book when you picked it up—it isn't *1001 Ways to Make Money* Guaranteed. It's *1001 Ways to Make Money* If You Dare.

> Dare \ 'der\ (verb): to challenge to perform an action especially as a proof of courage.

Source: Merriam-Webster Online.

That means all these entries aren't surefire ideas that will necessarily crank you out some cash. (This is a book after all, not an ATM.) Some are easier than others. Some are riskier than others. Some are more *risqué* than others. It's your choice to follow up on particular ones that pique your interest and pass over those that don't really fall within your self-assigned zone of "smart choices."

Think of it as a Choose Your Own Adventure, where every "See Page . . ." leads to a *real* adult choice in your *real* adult life. Enjoy!

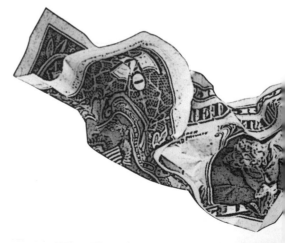

Introduction

BY TRENT HAMM

My father was the master of the "side hustle." When he got home from work, his day was really just beginning. He'd round up the family and before we knew it, we were doing something crazy, like baiting fishing lines, collecting aluminum cans, weeding gardens, brushing animal furs, popping open clam shells, and countless other interesting things.

Sure, along the way, our family made some money from these activities, but my memories don't rest on the fact that we were doing these things for money. I remember summer evenings with my father laughing as I sunk to my knees in a muddy garden. I remember him giving me a congratulatory slap on the back when I came up with a good idea to make a few dollars. I remember fishing expeditions at dawn, pulling in lines loaded with fish, and watching the sun rise over the still water. I remember organizing my aluminum can collecting schemes, finding new ways to maximize the cans collected while minimizing the work.

To put it simply, some of the most memorable moments of my life are tied around earning a few extra dollars in some of the craziest ways you can imagine. Sure, some of the things we tried didn't work. Sometimes, we'd come up with moneymaking schemes that were completely laughable. Other times, we'd find ourselves way over our heads in some crazy plan or another.

Many days, though, we would get really engaged with a new moneymaking plan and find ourselves enjoying the work—and the fact that we were building something that was really earning some solid money for the family together.

The most important part of the journey was that we were having a lot of fun together, filling lazy afternoons with a lot of laughter, a lot of memories, and on the best days, a few more dollars in our pockets.

1001 Ways to Make Money If You Dare is a lot like my childhood. The pages of this book are loaded with a lot of great ideas for earning a few extra dollars in your spare time. Many of them are quite fun. Some could earn you a nice sum of money. And others are included more to make you laugh at the idea of doing something so completely insane.

Whether you're looking for extra change, a laugh, or enough money to make a profound change in your life—this book's for you. Each entry is rated on a system that scores the endeavor's risk factor (☠ – ☠ ☠ ☠ ☠) as well as its potential monetary return (*$* – *$ $ $ $*).

Take this book, browse through the pages, and open yourself up to the sheer fun that a "side hustle" can bring. Try out a few of these tactics—and enjoy a good laugh at the idea of trying others.

CHAPTER 1

From the Comfort of Your Home

Each of these entries gives you an idea on how to scrape up some scratch without even having to change out of your pajamas. Some are rather simple, and others take a bit more fortitude to pull off. Read and repeat at your own risk.

1 START UP A DAY CARE. Who says kids aren't good for anything? You can make a nice nickel off the parents who work all day when you launch your very own Some Place Special—or some other equally comfortingly titled hot spot for tots. Your payout will depend on how many underage boarders you take in, as well as how risky this endeavor may be to your homestead (beware spilled juice, ransacked rooms, and finger-painted wallpaper).

☠ ☠   *$ $ $*   *tried it* ○

2 HAVE A TAG SALE. It's like eBay for the Internet-less. Rummage through your attic and cellar, go into those forgotten drawers, and finally make it to the back of your closet. Price everything out, slap sticky tags on all your wares, and hang up fliers throughout your neighborhood advertising your driveway department store (you might even send out a social-network blast on that new-fangled World Wide Web calling for all your friends to buy your crap).

☠   *$ $*   *tried it* ○

3 GET A ROOMMATE. Go ahead, admit it: You miss college. You miss sharing a cramped space with another human being who is at all times close enough for you to tell what type of toothpaste he uses. Now that you have a house (or apartment), you can take in a roomie to split the rent so you can actually pocket some of your paycheck rather than blowing it on your mortgage broker or landlord. Try getting a friend to move in, or if you really feel daring—throw an ad up on craigslist.

☠   *$ $*   *tried it* ○

4   **MOVE BACK IN WITH YOUR PARENTS.** Don't bother getting a roommate. Become a roommate. Depending on how much your parents love you, you may be able to freeload a roof over your head and food in your stomach. However, chances are that you'll have to put up some sort of boarding cost. But it will be a lot less than you're paying now—they're your parents after all. The only thing at risk is your sanity.

☠ ☠ $ $ *tried it* ○

5   **PIMP OUT YOUR PARKING SPOT.** You ride the bus, take the train, or pedal your ass to work. Why do you even have a driveway? Take advantage of the available asphalt and throw an ad up on the Net, or go old school and post it on telephone poles with "Interested? Call me." tabs. The harder it is to find on-street parking in your area, the more you can charge.

☠ $ $ $ *tried it* ○

6   **SCROUNGE FOR CHANGE.** Desperate times call for desperate measures. Turn over the couch cushions, check under the rug, dig through old pants' pockets. Do what you have to do to find your fair share of nickels, dimes, pennies, quarters, and—if you're lucky—a stray Sacagawea or two. Roll them up in those nifty papers you get from the bank (don't cop out and use those machines) and turn your findings into some crisp new bills.

☠ $ *tried it* ○

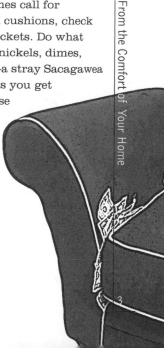

7 **RENT YOUR BIKE.** *Sweet Schwinn!* It's okay. We understand. The whole "be greener, be leaner—bike to work" New Year's resolution didn't work out. But now your Huffy's just taking up space and collecting dust in your basement. Take a page from the Danes and make your two-wheeler available to the public, for a price. The risk here is someone going *Pee-Wee's Big Adventure* on you and riding off into the sunset with your set of wheels.

☠ ☠ $ *tried it* ○

8 **MAIL OUT A CHAIN LETTER.** You're not taking advantage of your nearest and dearest—you're letting them in on the ground level of an upstart entrepreneurial enterprise. Compose a letter with instructions to return a single dollar to the five people on the enclosed list and then replace the bottom person with their own name and address (your name's on the top), and pass the list and instructions on to their friends and family. Careful: This is what that uptight government likes to call a "pyramid scheme."

☠ ☠ $ $ *tried it* ○

9 **REDEEM YOUR CANS AND BOTTLES.** Who says addictions don't pay off? Parlay your love for Diet Coke into cold harsh cash—a nickel in most states, ten cents for the right container in the right place (California and Michigan), and possibly nothing if your state doesn't believe in the whole "bottle bill" thing. Check your state laws before you rinse and sort. You wouldn't want to recycle for nothing.

☠ $ *tried it* ○

10 **CLEAN OUT YOUR CLOSET.** If you aren't up for a full-blown tag sale you can always resell right to consignment shops. It'd be in your best interest to wash and hang whatever you plan on selling. Presentation does matter when you try to haggle for an extra buck or two.

☠ $ $ *tried it* ○

11 **TURN YOUR BACKYARD INTO A "LOCATION."** How cool would it be if you received a party invite that listed the location as "[Your name here]'s backyard"? With a little sprucing up and some marketing, it could very well be the case. Offer to rent out your lawn space to friends for a fee so they can hold that garden soiree they always dreamed about. The risk comes the next morning when you're outside with a poker picking up trash.

☠ ☠ $ $ $ *tried it* ○

12 **RENT OUT YOUR HOUSE FOR A FUNCTION.** Take the fun indoors and allow others to use your spacious pad as a place for their own parties. (Note: Spacious, clean, and clear of empty pizza boxes is a prerequisite to this being pulled off.) The risk rises, though, when you allow others inside. Be sure to remove any breakables from heavily trafficked areas, and lock up whatever's concealable and worth stealing.

☠ ☠ ☠ $ $ $ *tried it* ○

13 **THROW A PARTY AND CHARGE ADMISSION.** If you're sick of everyone else having all the fun, organize your own shindig and have guests fork over a fee to get in. (Nothing says classy like a cover charge.) In order to make sure your guests will want to throw down to raise it up, you'll need to provide plenty of food and beverages. Just be sure your per-person overhead is covered by the ticket price.

☠ ☠ ☠ $ $ *tried it* ○

14 **CHARGE ENTRY TO A SUPER BOWL PARTY.** There are parties and then there are *Super Bowl* parties. However, you'll need the right setup to pull off making people pay to enjoy the big game. A huge (not big, but *huge*) television is necessary, as is surround sound and enough pork products, chips, and beer to put your neighborhood pub to shame. The risk may seem lower than a regular bash, as partygoers will be contained to one area, but if you ruin this once-a-year extravaganza, it's going to take a while to live it down.

☠ ☠ ☠ $ *tried it* ○

15 **HOST A SWINGER PARTY.** Bring some '70s sin back to your stuffy suburb by playing "keys in the fishbowl" with some willing participants (and their equally willing spouses). Ask for a discretionary "donation" upon entry and then let the martini sipping, Parcheesi playing, and partner swapping ensue. But be careful—on top of the typical party risks, this one tacks on broken marriages and sexually transmitted diseases.

☠ ☠ ☠ ☠ $ $ $ *tried it* ○

16 **PUT YOUR FURNITURE UP FOR SALE.** That old couch has plenty of memories planted in its squished springs, but now it's time to remind it who's boss by posting it on craigslist, the Facebook marketplace, or the good ol' print-and-paper classifieds. Just be sure to check between the cushions. You wouldn't want to risk missing some change-scrounging opportunities.

☠ $ $ *tried it* ○

17 **SELL YOUR TELEVISION.** Studies say television has led to the dumbing down of American society. Do your part and kick your set to the curb. And by *curb* we mean the most efficient resell outlet. The modern household has more TVs than a sports bar, so it's doubtful a single set will be missed.

☠ $ $ *tried it* ○

18 **CLEAR OUT YOUR KITCHEN FOR CASH.** Hate to break it to you, but chances are you're no Martha Stewart. Therefore your seven-cup food processor, melon baller, and tortilla press probably aren't seeing much action. The sooner you quiet that pretentious gourmet inside of you and see the amount of hardly used kitchenware you could hock online, the better.

☠   *$ $*   ***tried it*** ○

19 **PUT YOUR PAINTINGS UP FOR SALE.** Who needs decorated walls anyway? Channel your inner minimalist and transform your home into a stark, bare-wall world—and make a buck in the process. Use a high-resolution digital camera to take photos of your prints and originals for your craigslist or auction house ads. Just be careful: You never know when a "nobody" could turn into a "somebody" and that original you sold for a few dollars could retail for a few thousand.

☠ ☠   *$*   ***tried it*** ○

20 **GET CASH FOR YOUR VIDEO GAMES.** There are two ways to make a pretty penny reselling your video games. One is to beat or give up on the hot game of the moment and then put it up for sale online (or go to a used game shop and sell it to them). The other is to dig through your closets and attic to find cartridges that are in demand for older systems. (At the time of writing, a copy of *Mario Kart* for the N64 sells for upwards of $25 on eBay.)

☠   *$*   ***tried it*** ○

21 **TURN YOUR LIBRARY INTO A BOOKSTORE.** Usually, you buy a book, read the book, and then put it on your shelf to collect dust. What if it went more along the lines of—buy a book, read the book, and then put it on Amazon.com to collect some cash? Don't let your books collect dust. Make them collect dollars instead.

☠ $ *tried it* ○

22 **SELL YOUR STACK OF DVDS.** Honestly, how many times can you really watch *Notes on a Scandal* before it just gets creepy? Take an inventory of your movie collection and make "must have" and "must sell" piles. (And yes, *Cutthroat Island* goes in "must sell.") Create an account on a site like DVDPawn.com, or sell directly to other cinemaphiles using an auction site like eBay.

☠ $ *tried it* ○

23 **TIME TO TRADE IN YOUR TOOLS.** Think of how many times you've really used that belt sander or radial saw sitting in your garage. Go ahead. If it's less than the fingers on one hand (or if you're missing a finger on one hand because of your amateur woodshop), it's time to put them up for sale on any one of the resale sites. The risk increases here because if a home repair project comes up, you may need the specific tool you just hocked online—and you'll have to pay for a new one or to rent one.

☠ ☠ $ $ *tried it* ○

24 **SELL YOUR EXERCISE EQUIPMENT.** We get it—it was late one night, you were feeling bad about yourself, and you wanted to change. But now your Bowflex is sitting in the corner of your living room with the week's ironing hanging off its resistance arms. Not really what it's meant to be used for. Put your equipment up for sale on either craigslist or the Facebook marketplace. You don't want to worry about how you're going to ship this kind of stuff.

☠ $ $ *tried it* ○

25 **MAKE SOME MONEY OFF YOUR CHILDHOOD MEMORIES.**
Everyone gets all warm and fuzzy reminiscing about playing with a particular toy way back in the day. Do yourself
a favor and hunt down those playthings of yesteryear. You
may be sitting on a goldmine if you've got the right doll
or action figure. However, even if it isn't a first-generation, Pepsi-version of Optimus Prime (retailing on eBay
for $4,950), your once-prized possession could earn some
scratch from a nostalgic boomer or too-cool hipster.

☠ $ $ *tried it* ○

26 **DO MAILINGS FOR BUSINESSES.** Often the first to go in
times of economic trouble is a company's support staff. That
means menial tasks like mailings are left up to people who
have too much on their plate, and are most likely willing to
freelance out the work. Check listings on support service
sites, or show some initiative and contact local businesses
directly.

☠ $ *tried it* ○

27 **RENT YOUR COUCH.** It's true. Couch-surfing has become a
respectable way to see the world. (Respectable in the sense
that there are now websites dedicated to finding your ass a
cushion in cities across the world.) If you have some extra
space, a nice sofa, and don't mind a stranger crashing in
your pad—post your rate on AirBedandBreakfast.com.

☠ ☠ $ $ *tried it* ○

28 **HOST A FIGHT NIGHT.** Similar to the Super Bowl sugges-
tion, you need to make certain that your pad is properly
equipped before you go advertising a rowdy fight night.
The last thing you need is a bunch of people looking to
take in a good bruising when all you have is a twenty-
seven-inch Panasonic for the viewing. Be sure to factor in
the pay-per-view cost when setting the entry fee.

☠ ☠ ☠ $ $ *tried it* ○

From the Comfort of Your Home

29 **RUN A BEIRUT TOURNAMENT.** Take a trip back to your co-ed days, with cheap beer, loud music, and a friendly game of ten-cup beer pong. Charge each pair who wants to play, set up a bracket system, and see who comes out on top. Be sure to outline your house rules so there's no squabbling over reracking mid-turn, bouncing, and whether or not you can blow a ball out that isn't an outright sink.

☠ ☠ $ $ *tried it* ○

30 **RENT YOUR POOL.** Not everyone's lucky enough to have a pool in their backyard for those hot summer days and cool weekend barbecues. Therefore you can capitalize on demand. Whether you choose to charge per-person admission to your cement pond, or rent the whole thing out for a special event, be sure to get some sort of safety waiver signed—or else you may find yourself in the deep end.

☠ ☠ ☠ $ $ *tried it* ○

31 **HOST A POKER NIGHT.** Act as your very own casino owner and break out the card table for some hold 'em or five-card stud. Set your buy-ins and buy-ups with winner take all, and pocket a house fee for putting the whole thing on—the higher the stakes, the higher the fee. Who knows, maybe you'll even win and take the pot on top of the money you make holding the game.

☠ ☠ $ $ *tried it* ○

32   **GET PAID TO REVIEW PRODUCTS.** You bitch and moan when something doesn't work like it should, and you talk about how you couldn't live without something when it functions correctly. Why not make some money either trashing or praising that something. Check out Consumer Search.com and see if your assessment skills are good enough to help pay the bills.

☠   *$ $*   *tried it* ○

33   **WRITE TO STRANGERS FOR MONEY.** It can't hurt, right? If it works for that Nigerian prince who won't stop e-mailing you, then you might as well give it a try. Type up a letter that explains your story, why you're in need, what you'd do with the money, and so on. Then play white-page roulette and mail out a stack with a self-addressed stamped envelope (you don't want to seem *too* cheap, do you?).

☠   *$*   *tried it* ○

34   **SELL YOUR CELL.** In this text-message and Bluetooth world, a phone's "in" for about fifteen minutes. If you're the kind of person who needs to keep up with technology, chances are you have a drawer full of functioning cell phones. Put them up for purchase online. Some people don't care if their cell can send high-res videos or find them the nearest Italian restaurant.

☠   *$ $*   *tried it* ○

35   **GET MARRIED.** A quick way to (hopefully) double your assets and (undoubtedly) quadruple your headaches, marriage can work for you financially if you play up the "what's mine is yours, what's yours is mine" sentiment. As long as your future spouse isn't deep in debt, wedding bells will be *ka-ching*-ing.

☠ ☠   *$ $*   *tried it* ○

36   **GET DIVORCED.** While the goal— financially—for walking down the aisle is doubling up on your income and savings, the reason for divorce—besides those pesky irreconcilable differences—is to cut your losses and walk away with a nice severance package. The risk here is how much better your divorce lawyer is than your one-time soul mate's. As long as you don't get stuck footing the bill, your marital exit should put you in the black.

☠ ☠ ☠ $ $ *tried it* ○

37   **CHARGE TO RECORD SHOWS FOR OTHERS.** Some people have TiVo. Some people have DVR. Some people have to record the ol' fashioned way. And most of those people end up messing up their recordings because they don't know how to do it. Here's a perfect opportunity for you. Set up gigs recording television shows and special events for the tech-incompetent. The money might not be much, but as long you know what you're doing, the hassle isn't either.

☠ $ *tried it* ○

38   **SELL YOUR GOLD.** Turn over your jewelry box and dump out its contents. That earring that doesn't have a match— guess what? You're not going to find the other one. That chain that's knotted beyond untangling? Don't bother. That watch with the cracked face and broken clasp? Time to give it up. Send whatever mismatched, broken, and unwanted pieces of gold jewelry you have in to one of those cash-for-gold operations, or go to your friendly neighborhood pawnshop.

☠ $ $ *tried it* ○

39 **SELL YOUR SILVER.** Forever runner-up to its yellow precious-metal counterpart, reselling your silver can net you just as much cash as selling your gold. So whether you decide to hock that gaudy bauble of an anniversary gift, those candlesticks from Nana, or that contested silver medal you won while juicing—it's up to you. Why settle for second best when you can have a fistful of ones?

☠ $ $ *tried it* ○

40 **RENT YOUR CAR.** Who needs Zipcar when they have *you*? You're sitting on your couch watching a *Law & Order* marathon. You're not going anywhere. Why not let someone else take your wheels for a spin? Set an hourly rate and get the assignment of responsibilities in writing (gas, repair costs, etc.). The nicer your car, though, the riskier it is letting someone else behind the wheel.

☠ ☠ $ $ *tried it* ○

41 **CASH IN YOUR CAR.** Maybe all this renting out of your coupe makes you realize that you don't actually need it. If that's the case, put that sucker up for sale. You have a few options. You can park it in front of your house with a "For Sale" sign in the window, put an ad online, or sell it to a used car lot. It's probably best to ballpark the return on each based on your particular ride before deciding.

☠ $ $ $ *tried it* ○

42 **LAUNCH A MOVIE RENTAL BUSINESS.** In the same spirit of becoming Mom 'n Pop Zipcar, cash in on another financially sound entrepreneurial enterprise—the direct-to-mail movie rental business. If you have a big enough DVD library and the wherewithal to keep up with mailing out requests, put your catalog out to the masses and see who bites. Just be sure to undercut the competition, while keeping rental costs high enough to cover mailings.

☠ $ *tried it* ○

43 **TURN YOUR HOME INTO A FILM SET.** How cool would it be to watch actors chew the scenery—and have that scenery be your house? It could happen. All you have to do is take some pictures of your home and post them on a site like FilmingLocations.com. If a location scout thinks your house has the chops to be in the pictures, it could become a star. Beware though, if the film gets a cult following, you may get some film geeks standing outside reciting lines at all hours of the night.

☠ ☠ $ $ $ *tried it* ○

44 **HOST YOUR OWN HAPPY HOUR.** All you need is some booze, some snacks, and some friends. You can buy the alcohol and the appetizers, but since you're expecting to make money off these people—you can't buy your buddies. So before you hit up the discount liquor store, make sure you have a head count that covers the overhead. Charge a small cover, shake up some cocktails, and make Friday afternoons at your place the most fun part of the weekend.

☠ $ *tried it* ○

45 **START YOUR OWN MUSEUM.** Everyone is an authority on something—be it bees, boxing, or bullshit. Parlay your authority on a topic and collection of all related materials into a cultural center for the world to see. (And by world, we mean anyone who's bored or who has an equally high affinity for whatever you're curating.)

☠ $ *tried it* ○

46 **TURN YOUR BACKYARD INTO A PARKING LOT.** Maybe you live close to a ballpark, concert venue, or other area of mass interest where parking is a pain—or costs a fortune. Get yourself some cones and a sign, underprice the competing lots, and be prepared for your beautiful lawn to turn into a mud bowl.

☠ ☠ $ $ *tried it* ○

47 **CREATE YOUR OWN CAMPGROUND.** What sounds more adventurous than a weekend away in the wilderness—at Bob's Backyard. If you own enough land located in a nice enough location, you could be Bob. It's best to check on state regulations if you plan on going legit, but if you just want to let a few hippies pitch a tent for a couple nights, we won't tell anyone.

☠ ☠   *$ $*   *tried it* ○

48 **RUN A ROADSIDE ATTRACTION.** Similar to starting your own museum, running a roadside attraction banks on people's curiosity. Maybe you've taught your roaches how to race around a track, have collected and combined spit-balls to create the world's largest lump of paper and saliva, or have stuffed and positioned enough squirrels to reenact the opening scenes to all of Shakespeare's plays. Whatever it is, market the attraction on the side of the highway and charge people to come take a look.

☠   *$*   *tried it* ○

49 **START A SWEAR JAR.** What better way to teach the people you live with to speak respectfully than to charge them up the ass for using four-letter words? Make sure the penalties are known, and then do your best at policing the foul language. However, there's a big risk here, if your own mouth puts sailors and truckers to shame. The point is to make money—not to lose it. Stick some soap in your mouth and hope for the best.

☠ ☠ ☠   *$*   *tried it* ○

50 **HOST A CONCERT SERIES.** Know any emerging musicians? Charge less than the local coffee shop does and you've got yourself a concert series out of the comfort of your own home. Charge extra for any advertising you do like putting up fliers.

☠   *$ $*   *tried it* ○

51 **HOST A MUSIC FESTIVAL.** Bonnaroo? Overrated. Coachella? Too commercial. Your very first music fest? Totally rad (or whatever the kids are saying these days). Line up some local talent, put together a makeshift stage, and be ready for a weekend of acoustic guitars, chicks with dreadlocks, and free lovin'. Your backyard will never be the same.

☠ ☠ ☠   *$ $ $*   *tried it* ○

52 **HOST A CHILDREN'S PLAYHOUSE.** Frazzled parents constantly look for new places to drop their kids for a few hours. If your place is kid-friendly, offer it up as a playhouse for a few hours on the weekends. Pay some high schoolers minimum wage to watch the wee ones and you're all set.

☠ ☠   *$ $*   *tried it* ○

53 **BE A "MANNY."** Women sick of their husbands sleeping with the nanny are the first to jump on board the new trend of hiring male nannies, or "mannies" as they are so lovingly referred to as. Cash in if you're a dude by getting in touch with your sensitive child-loving side by registering with a nanny service or advertising your skills online.

☠ ☠   *$ $ $*   *tried it* ○

54 **HOST AN EXCHANGE STUDENT.** Introduce an unsuspecting foreigner to the customs of Americans by cashing in on programs for housing visiting students. For extra cash, get the student to tutor language students out of your house and skim some off the top.

☠ ☠   *$ $*   *tried it* ○

55 **TAKE IN A FOSTER CHILD.** It's the ultimate selfless act that you get paid for. There are tons of kids out there looking for a loving home. Have an extra room? Feeling lonely since you became an empty nester? Visit *www.adopting.org* for more information.

☠ ☠ ☠   *$ $*   *tried it* ○

56 **SELL YOUR SHOES.** They say you can't really know a man until you've walked a mile in his shoes. Give someone that opportunity by selling your footwear. You really only need one pair, so say adios to the rest (yes, even that blue suede pair you keep waiting for an occasion to wear).

☠   *$ $*   *tried it* ○

57 **HOST A FUND-RAISER.** Nonprofits need cheap places to host fundraisers so that they can put as much of the proceeds as possible to the organization. If you charge less than the local Holiday Inn ballroom you're golden.

☠   *$*   *tried it* ○

58 **HOST AN AUCTION.** Auctions aren't just happening online. If you have a big room in your house and some folding chairs, you can host an auction for a local antique store or a nonprofit. To make some extra bucks, offer your services as an auctioneer.

☠   *$ $*   *tried it* ○

59 **RUN A HAUNTED HOUSE.** Grab some peeled grapes (eyeballs), cold spaghetti (brains), and hot dogs (intestines) and you've got yourself the start of a haunted house. Replace all of the bulbs in your home with red and black lights and make sure to rig up a couple of severed heads to fall when doors are opened.

☠ ☠   *$*   *tried it* ○

60 **ENTER RADIO CONTESTS.** Use those free nights and week-end minutes to call radio stations over and over and over and over again until you win. Don't like the prize? Sell it on eBay or craigslist—at an inflated price of course.

☠   *$ $*   *tried it* ○

61 **RENT OUT YOUR KARAOKE MACHINE.** Remember that karaoke machine you got for Christmas last year that's been in its box ever since? Rent it out to tone-deaf fiends who don't have their own. Better yet, have a karaoke party and charge people per song (once they've had a chance to drink away their stage fright).

☠ ☠   *$ $*   *tried it* ○

62 **HOST SEX TOY PARTIES.** Are your friends underserved in the bedroom? Help a sister out by hosting a sex toy party so that they can buy some bedroom fun without the embarrassing trip to an adult store. They get their toys, you get your cut, and everybody goes home happy.

☠ ☠   *$ $*   *tried it* ○

63 **MAKE MOONSHINE.** Whatever you do, don't sell that gin tub; there isn't quite the same market for homemade "juice" as there was during Prohibition, but that doesn't mean you can't still cash in. Troll the Internet for tips on perfecting your own recipe—and remember, people love the appeal of a secret ingredient.

☠ ☠ ☠ ☠   *$ $*   *tried it* ○

64 **CHARGE FOR SLEDDING.** If there is a mondo hill anywhere on your property, you've got an instant way of making cash (assuming you live somewhere where it snows—sorry Arizonians). For some extra cash you can also rent out sleds, charge for use of your bathroom, and sell hot cocoa (spiked for the parents).

☠ ☠   *$ $*   *tried it* ○

65 **SELL YOUR COMIC BOOKS.** How many times has someone proclaimed "nerd!" when walking into your house? Yeah, it's time to get rid of those comic books. Don't get hosed though; if someone offers to buy them all for a lump sum make sure there aren't any gems hiding in the pile before forking them over.

☠   *$ $*   *tried it* ○

66 **SELL MEMENTOS.** Love that dated "baby's first Christmas" ornament you've been holding on to? So would someone else your age who's ornaments all got lost in a move or destroyed by a fire. Make your mementos someone else's by hawking them on eBay. You can always make new memories with your new money.

☠ ☠   *$ $*   *tried it* ○

67 **FIND AND SELL SPORTS MEMORABILIA.** This doesn't just mean autographs, balls, and jerseys. Get creative—locks of hair, used chewing gum, and jock straps have all been known to sell for crazy amounts of money to crazy people.

☠ ☠   *$ $ $*   *tried it* ○

68 **TRANSCRIBE AUDIOTAPES.** Mundane tasks like transcribing audiotapes need to be done by somebody, so why not you? If you get really good, you can even multitask and watch TV while you're typing—just make sure to review before submitting for any errors or subliminal messages that found their way into the doc.

☠   *$ $*   *tried it* ○

69 **KEY IN HARD COPY DOCUMENTS.** While many of the typist jobs are being outsourced these days, you can still find plenty of people (especially closeted technophobes and people with awful keyboard skills) willing to pay to have their handwritten documents typed up.

☠   *$*   *tried it* ○

70 **START A BED AND BREAKFAST.** If you have an extra room or two and can whip up a respectable breakfast, you can open a B&B. What else are you going to do with your kids' rooms now that they're gone? Throw in bonus things like a guided tour of your city to bring in even more dough.

☠ ☠ $ $ $ *tried it* ○

71 **RENT OUT YOUR BOAT.** You know that boat that you're still making payments on? Why not let someone help you out with those payments by renting it whenever you're not using it. Make sure you get the renter to put down a security deposit in case any damage is done.

☠ ☠ $ $ $ *tried it* ○

72 **RENT YOUR PET.** Old people, college students, and spouses of allergy-inflicted people often long for the love of a furry little creature. If you've got one, you can cash in by renting it out. The cuter the animal, the more money you can charge for an hour in its company.

☠ $ $ *tried it* ○

73 **SELL SOIL.** Your lawn is full of soil. Need extra cash? Sell it. You weren't using it anyway, so it might as well go to the highest paying gardener looking to score some extra dirt for her new greenhouse.

☠ $ $ *tried it* ○

74 **SELL COMPOST.** Some people are too lazy (or afraid of the smell) to compost. But that doesn't mean that they don't want the benefits the rotting material brings. Buy a compost pail for your kitchen and put all of your vegetable and fruit-based scraps in. Take it outside when it's full and before long you'll have your very own compost heap. Try selling to neighbors before branching out, since compost isn't very portable.

☠ ☠ $ *tried it* ○

75 **SELL CAR PARTS.** Instead of junking your broken-down ride, consider whether any of the parts might make you some cash. Don't just trust the local mechanic, who might try to scam you by taking it apart himself after giving you $10 for the whole thing—get on the Web and post parts on auction sites.

☠ ☠ $ $ *tried it* ○

76 **HOST A POETRY SLAM.** Ask the owners of bars you frequent about slow nights like Tuesdays or Wednesdays. If you can pack in the people, chances are you can work out getting a cut of the profits. And hey, people love poetry slams!

☠ ☠ $ $ *tried it* ○

77 **CREATE AND RENT OUT A DARK ROOM.** Chances are you have at least one room in your house with no windows. Do you really need that second bathroom? Put it to use by renting it out to a local photographer with no dark space of his own.

☠ $ $ *tried it* ○

78 **HOST AN OPEN STUDIO EVENT.** Artists don't always live or work in the most appealing places. So they often need a place that people are actually willing to go to where they can showcase their work. Throw out a cheese plate and charge the artist either a flat fee or percentage of profits made (depending on how pricey and aesthetically pleasing the art is).

☠ $ $ *tried it* ○

79 **RUN AN ARTIST RETREAT.** Artists like to get together to get creative. This is especially lucrative if you live near woods—there's something about connecting to nature that artists, especially those who live in the city, seem to love.

☠ $ $ *tried it* ○

80 **RENT A ROOM AS AN ART STUDIO.** Most artists are used to being creative in adverse conditions—hey, whatever helps get the creative juices flowing, right? So chances are they won't mind painting in your noninsulated sunroom during the winter, or in the dark windowless basement room that you never got around to finishing.

☠ ☠ $ $ $ *tried it* ○

CHAPTER 2

Hittin' the Streets

While you won't need to cue up the Bee Gees and strut like John Travolta, getting off your couch, out of your house, and hitting the pavement opens up a world of opportunity for making money. Take the lead from these inventive ideas and see what type of return you can achieve by taking it to the streets.

81 **COLLECT BOTTLES.** Earn green and go green at the same time. People throw away bottles every day, and you can profit to the tune of five or ten cents per bottle. To make the most amount of money possible, find out where the biggest parties are and pick through the trash the next day. You may look homeless, but you'll be rolling in the dough.

☠ ☠ $ $ *tried it* ○

82 **SELL SCRAP METAL.** All you have to do is collect simple items like the wires on electronic equipment, car batteries, bedsprings, storm doors, and the like. Sure, your friends may be wondering why their TV won't turn on and their beds are lumpy, but at least you'll be able to pay your bills. Find a scrap dealer in your area at *www.recycleinme.com.*

☠ ☠ $ $ $ *tried it* ○

83 **GO SCAVENGING.** One person's trash is another's treasure. This should be your motto while searching the city dump for anything that you can sell. Used car parts, old couches, clothing . . . everything is up for grabs. You may need to wash—or fumigate—what you find, but you can sell it to a car mechanic or a consignment shop for profit. Talk about found money!

☠ $ $ $ *tried it* ○

84 **HUNT FOR COPPER PIPING.** The price for scrap copper has risen over 400 percent in the past three years, which means that you can make a pretty penny collecting it. Copper is found in air-conditioning units, refrigerators, and plumbing. We don't advise taking it out of items that are still working—unless you want your roommate to kill you. You can also find scrap copper dealers by logging onto *www.recycleinme.com.*

☠ ☠ $ $ $ *tried it* ○

85 **HEAD OUT WITH A METAL DETECTOR.** We're all familiar with the image of a beach bum searching a beautiful beach with his trusty metal detector. Looks fun, doesn't it? You probably won't be able to retire on what you find, but you never know. Modern metal detectors even have alert sensors that let you know what's down there before you spend an hour scooping sand.

☠   **$**   *tried it* ◯

86 **SEARCH FOR BURIED TREASURE.** Leave the metal detector behind and try to locate where X marks the spot. Whether it's swashbuckling pirates, or greedy pioneers, there are tons of local legends about lost riches. In case you're not lucky enough to stumble upon a treasure map *Goonies*-style, hit the area library and research what forgotten fortunes you might be able to find.

☠ ☠   **$ $ $**   *tried it* ◯

87 **GO ANTIQUING.** We've all seen an episode of *Antiques Roadshow* where a woman brings in an old, wobbly wooden chair that turns out to be worth eight trillion dollars. Make this premise work for you by frequenting local yard sales, antique stores, and auctions. Have everything you find appraised, and, for God's sake, don't repaint, stain, or sand anything. You never know how much value that original coat of ugly green paint may add.

☠   **$ $ $**   *tried it* ◯

88 **COLLECT GREASE.** Restaurant owners are sitting on a gold mine. Cooking grease has now become a hot commodity to make bio-diesel fuel. Offer to dispose of the waste product for restaurateurs who don't know that they're cooking up a profit—and letting it slip through their slick fingers.

☠   **$ $**   *tried it* ◯

89 **PICK UP ROADKILL.** Roadkill cleanup is a sad, messy, smelly business, but it can also be a profitable one! How much you make depends on your location and how strong your stomach is. Many highway departments will pay you for cleanup. A creative alternative is to taxidermy any animal you find and sell it for a neat profit. Or you can sell fresh roadkill to any hunter looking to impress his friends.

☠ ☠ $ $ *tried it* ○

90 **FIND AN OIL FIELD.** You, Inc. would be a way better oil contributor than any of the "Big Five." The only issue here is finding a source. This might get dangerous because all the spots for lucrative domestic drilling have either been snatched up or are protected by that pesky Department of the Interior. In order to stake a claim to land that's a cash cow, you'll have to travel to the Middle East or South America—which might get a *little* dangerous.

☠ ☠ ☠ ☠ $ $ $ $ *tried it* ○

91 **PANHANDLE—WITH A TWIST.** In this awful economy, the competition among beggars is intense. You need a special technique to earn money from the passers-by. Bet that the person you are asking can't solve a riddle and make it impossible to answer.

☠ ☠ $ *tried it* ○

92 **HOLD A CHALK ART SHOW.** We've all seen those amazing 3-D chalk drawings online. Now, put your skills to the test and earn some easy cash. Grab your little sister's sidewalk chalk, hit the pavement, and draw away! Advertise your "avant-garde" art show to a local college or art school. After all, college kids love experimental art. Best part of hosting this type of an art show? Easy cleanup!

☠ $ $ *tried it* ○

93 **PUT ON A PUPPET SHOW.** Puppets are "in" these days. RollingStone.com reports that even Kanye West is getting in on the action, working with Comedy Central to produce a show called *Boots* "[that] will feature felt characters rapping." Jump on the bandwagon and put on your own impromptu show. Socks with buttons for eyes don't cost a lot, and you'll reap the rewards.

☠ $ *tried it* ○

94 **WRITE YOUR OWN ONE-MAN SHOW.** Are you funny? Dramatic? Don't be shy. Head out to your local park and be prepared to wow the crowd. Have your friends collect money from the crowd while you showcase your acting prowess. Legitimize your show by posting fliers inviting everyone you can think of. Props won't hurt either.

☠ $ $ *tried it* ○

95 ***WOW* AS A STREET MAGICIAN.** Are you ready to work your magic—and earn some moolah? Find a place with a lot of people (preferably kids—especially if you're not that good) and put out your tip cup. Beware. Some cities require street performers to be licensed. If you don't get a license, wear good running shoes. After all, one of the best tricks a street magician can perform is a disappearing act.

☠ ☠ ☠ $ $ *tried it* ○

96 **BEGIN BREAK DANCING.** Get down and get paid. Break dancing began in the early 1970s and even today there's something about it that catches people's attention—and convinces them to open their wallets. People are even more likely to put their change in your coffer if you have a friend willing to battle with you. Have your audience bet on a winner . . . then split your winnings.

☠ ☠ $ $ *tried it* ○

Hittin' the Streets

97 **MIME FOR MONEY.** Let's face it. Mime's are creepy, but love 'em or hate 'em, you can make money by becoming one. At some point during your life, you've probably pretended you were stuck in a box or were going down an escalator. Take these party tricks, bring them to the street, and rake in the dough—just make sure you do it quietly.

☠ $ *tried it* ○

98 **BECOME A STREET PERFORMER.** Can you breathe fire? Lift heavy things with your little finger? Stand perfectly still for long periods of time? If so, you have some serious cash coming your way. Tourists—and locals for that matter—love watching people do weird things and will reward you for your odd talent. Many cities require performers to be licensed, so check to make sure you're not breaking any laws—unless you want to.

☠ ☠ $ *tried it* ○

99 **JUGGLE.** Put your coordination skills to work. Juggling is something that many people try, but few can successfully manage to do. If you know how to juggle—or are a fast learner—give this a try. Just be sure not to hit anyone with a flaming bowling pin. To learn more about juggling, go to *www.juggling.org.*

☠ ☠ $ *tried it* ○

100 **EXERCISE YOUR VOCAL CORDS.** Singing on the street is a surefire moneymaker. You don't even have to be good at it. Look at William Hung. As long as you put yourself—and your tip cup—out there, and aren't embarrassed by your lack of talent, you're good to go!

☠ $ *tried it* ○

101 **PLAY ON THE STREET CORNER.** You have your acoustic guitar shined and ready for strumming, have memorized all of Leonard Cohen's songs to seduce the ladies (or at the very least, you can play "Cars" by Gary Numan), and have picked out the busiest spot for pedestrian traffic. It's time to let the spotlight (or streetlight) shine and make some coin. Try writing some new lyrics about economic despair and set them to a familiar tune. Nothing gets the crowd going more than desperation.

☠   *$ $*   *tried it* ○

102 **BE A LIVING STATUE.** Do you have the desire to freak out strangers *and* make money? Well, acting as a living statue is your golden ticket. Wear a costume and put on makeup so you look like you're a statue, then stand on an elevated platform and move in slow motion in a way that makes sense with your costume.

☠ ☠   *$*   *tried it* ○

103 **GO DOOR TO DOOR TAKING SURVEYS.** Are you friendly? Outgoing? Not afraid of rejection? A job as a survey taker may be right for you. The premise is simple: knock on doors and convince people to answer questions about their lives. A bit of advice though—if the sign on the fence says "Beware of Dog," it's probably a good idea to walk on by that particular house.

☠   *$*   *tried it* ○

104 **JOIN A FOCUS GROUP.** You have strong opinions; why not get paid to express them! Marketing specialists all over the country are waiting to hear your thoughts on TV shows, juice drinks, and more. Check local craigslist postings for such opportunities.

☠   *$ $*   *tried it* ○

105 **SCALP TICKETS.** Everyone wants tickets to the big game. Help them achieve that goal while padding your pockets. All you need to be a scalper is a ticket—one that you can sell for five times its original price. Get yourself down to the ballpark, stadium, or playhouse, but keep a low profile. In most places, scalping is illegal.

☠ ☠ ☠   *$ $ $*   *tried it* ○

106 **BECOME A FREELANCE LIMO DRIVER.** Earn some extra cash and show up in style. This job is a little like being a hired gun. You drive the car, make some money, and keep the tip, but you're not actually employed by the company. The bad news: you have to wear a suit to work. The good news: nice pay for a few hours of work and a chance to hob-nob with the rich . . . and maybe famous.

☠   *$ $ $*   *tried it* ○

107 **HIRE YOURSELF OUT FOR AIRPORT RIDES.** You have a car. You know how to get the airport. Why not combine these skills and start your own business? Piece of advice: You'll get a bigger tip if you clean the fast food bags and coffee cups out the back of your car.

☠   *$ $*   *tried it* ○

108 **WORK AS A VALET.** If you can't afford a nice car, you may as well drive someone else's. Where else do you have the opportunity to drive a Porsche, BMW, and a Bentley all in one night? Find a valet job in your area at *http:// valetparkingjobs.jobamatic.com.*

☠   *$ $*   *tried it* ○

109 **WIN BAR TRIVIA.** Nothing sounds better than earning money while drinking a few beers! Many bars and restaurants now are hosting trivia nights where winners can earn money, gift certificates, and other prizes. Check out *www.nationaltrivia.com* to find a bar near you.

☠ $ *tried it* ○

110 **HOST BAR TRIVIA.** Why bother competing when you can run the show? Not only do you get to make snarky asides and comment on others' out-of-left-field answers, you also get paid. It's like you're a local Alex Trebek. Just don't let the power go to your head. Check out the websites for area companies that run pub trivia and apply to be an emcee.

☠ ☠ $ $ *tried it* ○

111 **SELL PONCHOS.** Take advantage of others' ignorance of the weather forecast—and their desperation when they get caught in the rain. For the days it's really pouring, you can even hike up the price. It's amazing what people will pay to stay dry.

☠ $ $ *tried it* ○

112 **OPEN UP AN UMBRELLA STAND.** Global warming is causing drastic weather changes—and an opportunity for you to profit. Sudden showers often catch pedestrians by surprise, and they're likely willing to shell out some cash to make sure they don't end up all wet. Stake out a spot in a high-end area. Those people definitely won't want their designer duds getting drenched.

☠ $ $ *tried it* ○

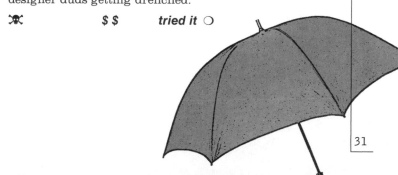

113 **BE A COMPANION TO AN ELDERLY PERSON.** Use the fact that you were always your grandparents' favorite to your advantage (and not just to incite your siblings). Along with just being a friend, you can also help the senior citizens in your care with their cooking and cleaning. And if you play your cards right, you may even get in the will.

☠ $ $ $ *tried it* ○

114 **SHINE SHOES.** Fortunately for you, businessmen still don't realize how inexpensive it is to buy shoe polish and do it at home. (And with the way they've recently run their businesses, are you surprised?) Take advantage of their stupidity and either set up a street stand or a home business.

☠ $ $ *tried it* ○

115 **PICK UP A GRAVEYARD SHIFT.** Has your dire debt caused you sleepless nights? Cash in on your insomnia by working all hours of the day. And if you get an unsupervised job, you can sleep at your leisure. (Don't blame us if your lack of sleep might lead to you starting a fight club.)

☠ ☠ $ $ $ *tried it* ○

116 **WORK AS A DAY LABORER.** Know that corner that contractors and crew supervisors drop by every morning? Go there. This form of not-so-legal labor will teach you a thing or two about hard work—and make you thankful for PowerPoint and Excel.

☠ ☠ ☠ $ $ *tried it* ○

117 **BE A COURIER.** With businesses now getting hip to the green trend, take out your bike and start delivering urgent packages around town. It even doubles as exercise! However, watch out for car doors flying open right as you pass them—you'll have trouble making money as a hospital's patient.

☠ ☠ $ $ *tried it* ○

118   **BECOME A PAPERBOY.** We're talking old school here, but with your car, you can make triple the money you made when you were fifteen. You're also better equipped to run away from dogs, look for new customers, and beg for tips.

☠ $ *tried it* ○

119   **DELIVER PIZZAS.** We know. It's hard to go back to something you did when you were in high school, but even in a bad economy, people gotta eat. Want to be especially daring? Make the pizza yourself—people will never know that it's not delivery, it's DiGiorno! This way, you keep all the money you bring in.

☠ $ $ *tried it* ○

120   **CLEAN OUT COINS FROM FOUNTAINS.** Since you were a young child, you have always fantasized about jumping in a public fountain and going on a coin-grabbing frenzy. It's okay—you can admit it. Now you can fulfill your dream while looting the coins meant to fulfill the dreams of others. Just be careful: You never know when someone will alert the cops to your coin cleanup.

☠ ☠ ☠ $ *tried it* ○

121   **BE AN ICE ROAD TRUCKER.** You've hauled commercial truckloads across the country but still desire a little more danger in your life. When you become an ice road trucker, you'll be the Jason Bourne of the road (or rather, the ice). Check out companies that hire truckers for the eighteen-wheel artic adventure like Nuna Logistics (*www.nuna logistics.com*).

☠ ☠ ☠ ☠ $ $ $ *tried it* ○

122 **SOLVE A CRIME FOR A REWARD.** You have watched enough *CSI* and *Law & Order* to know everything there is to know about any crime ever committed. So do your best Veronica Mars impression and get to the bottom of cases both small and large—and always for a fee.

☠ ☠ ☠ $ $ *tried it* ○

123 **LEAD A WALKING TOUR.** Is there anything interesting about the city that you live in? Maybe fitness-minded people would like to discover these things by foot. And trust me, by foot is the best way of doing it (if you've ever seen people try to navigate a busy city on Segways then you know what I mean).

☠ $ $ *tried it* ○

124 **LEAD A BICYCLE TOUR.** If you haven't already rented your bike to make money (see entry 7) then you can put it to use by leading a bicycle tour of your city. Buy a couple of beaters to fix up, and then you can double your money by both renting the bikes and leading the tour. It's so green!

☠ ☠ $ $ *tried it* ○

125 **SELL TOURIST MAPS.** Whether you simply pick up some stock maps or design and print your own, as long as you market them as "insider info" then you'll be all set. Throw a few gold stars on your area's main attractions as well as some green ones on "local favorites." Hit the street corner and start picking out people with cameras around their necks and mixed expressions of wonder and bewilderment.

☠ ☠ $ *tried it* ○

126 **GIVE TOURS OF STARS' HOMES.** Know the neighborhoods of the rich and famous? Or perhaps you're privy to the fact that some stars own vacation homes in your quaint little town (you know *them*—always trying to "get away from it all"). Whatever the case, charge some cash to guide people through the abodes of A-listers (or less money if all you know are the whereabouts of D-listers' duplexes).

☠ ☠ $ $ *tried it* ○

127 **LEAD A HAUNTED TOUR.** Set up tours that showcase all of your town's scary stories. If your city lacks interesting urban legends, you can always make some up. As long as you lead the tours in the dark with a flashlight shining on your face, the tourists will *have* to believe you.

☠ ☠ $ *tried it* ○

128 **TAKE PHOTOS OF TOURISTS.** Are you sick of tourists making a mockery of your historical landmarks? Well, there's not much you can do about that (besides giving them wrong directions); however, you can profit off their infatuation for having their picture taken. Just hang out there, take their picture for a profit, and bite your tongue.

☠ $ $ *tried it* ○

129 **BECOME A PAPARAZZO.** You have a penchant for taking pictures, but can't seem to make any cash off of your captures. Maybe's time to ditch your conscience and that hunt for credibility. Lose the 'tude, you Leibovitz wannabe, and start snapping shots for *US Weekly*, *In Touch*, and the *National Enquirer*. All you have to risk is your integrity—and getting punched in the face by Russell Crowe.

☠ ☠ ☠ $ $ $ *tried it* ○

130 **SELL YOUR BALLOON SCULPTURES.** Internet sites like *www.balloonmodels.com* provide you with instructional videos on how to create balloon animals. Put up ads on craigslist to be the entertainment at people's next party. The only drawback is becoming addicted to using your helium machine to make your voice high.

☠ ☠ $ $ *tried it* ○

131 **FACE PAINT FOR A FEE.** Young kids are suckers for face paint, and you can profit off of their love of looking like cats. Set up a station outside of local schools or in the park, but be careful that you don't look sketchy. (We highly recommend the face painting be done out in the open.)

☠ ☠ $ $ *tried it* ○

132 **CHARGE FOR CARICATURES.** Bring out your (money-making) artistic side. Set up a stand in the tourist-heavy part of your town and charge people money to point out their physical insecurities. Warning: Someone who doesn't understand "self-deprecation" might try to attack you.

☠ ☠ $ *tried it* ○

CHAPTER 3

Behind Your Computer

Reader84: i'm broke :-(

1001WAY$: Stop complaining and DO something about it.

Reader84: wut can i do?

1001WAY$: First of all, read this chapter . . . and secondly, stop looking at so much damn porn.

133 **BLOG FOR DOLLARS.** Do you want to get paid to blog about stuff you love? Check out *www.weblogsinc.com.* All you have to do is fill out a brief survey, already have a blog up and running, and they will contact you if you fit a position they have. Instead of spending hours talking about what you and your cat did the night before, you can make money writing about cats.

☠   *$ $*   *tried it* ○

134 **BLIND LINK FOR MONEY.** How many times have you been reading a blog and clicked on a link randomly left in the comments section? A lot? Don't worry, you're not alone. This is guerrilla marketing. Companies and entrepreneurs are willing to shell out cash for people to target sites where their consumers flock and leave links. Check out the gig board on craigslist, or contact small companies directly with an offer they can't refuse.

☠   *$*   *tried it* ○

135 **MODERATE AN ONLINE FORUM.** There are chat rooms for every subject imaginable. They need people to make sure there are no pedophiles lurking and that everyone is follow-ing the rules of the chat room. Pick a forum you're inter-ested in and get in touch with the "forum master."

☠   *$ $*   *tried it* ○

136 **BUY UP DOMAIN NAMES.** Every website needs a domain name. Purchase any addresses you think people or compa-nies might want to buy in the future. They're fairly cheap, $10–$40, just be sure to maintain the site so it isn't seen as e-squatting.

☠ ☠   *$ $*   *tried it* ○

137 **BUY AT DISCOUNT; RESELL AT RETAIL.** Dollar stores are full of items that are perfectly good; they just have been discontinued or are out of season. If they are specialty items, people will still pay the retail price. Take a trip to a discount store and pick up some high-end products and resell them online.

☠ $ $ *tried it* ○

138 **SELL OFFICE SUPPLIES ONLINE.** Is your home office turning into an Office Max? Do you collect office supplies and let them sit in your desk drawer for all eternity? Clean out your desk and sell the extra supplies online. You really don't need twenty bottles of Wite-Out.

☠ $ $ *tried it* ○

139 **TELECOMMUTE WHILE AT WORK.** If you get caught, you might be fired, so watch out with this one. However, if you're the king or queen of multitasking, you're in the clear. Do something simple that won't take a lot of time from your "real job," and keep your eyes peeled for nosy bosses.

☠ ☠ ☠ ☠ $ $ $ *tried it* ○

140 **SELL TEXTBOOKS.** Admit it, you'll never open that copy of *Western Civilization, Vol. 1* or *The Complete Works of Shakespeare* again. Since textbooks are so expensive on campus, sell yours on Amazon or even craigslist.

☠ $ $ *tried it* ○

141 **SELL YOUR EXTRA COMPUTER.** If you recently upgraded your system and no longer need that Mac from 1998, sell it online. People will always pick up old computers, even if it's just to ransack it for parts.

☠ $ $ *tried it* ○

142 **CONDUCT ONLINE GENEALOGY.** With websites like Ancestry.com and Familytree.com, finding family members is easy. Many people want to find out where they came from, so market yourself as someone who can help them track down their lineage.

☠ $ $ *tried it* ○

143 **PLAN OTHER PEOPLE'S TRIPS.** Become a one-person travel agency and find customers the best deals possible. Not everyone has time to plan their vacation, but they want it to be cheap and memorable. Take some classes about the travel industry and start today. Just remember, it's your ass if they don't have any fun!

☠ ☠ $ $ *tried it* ○

144 **WORK AS A TYPIST.** Many companies outsource small jobs like typing documents. You could even advertise your services at local colleges for those lazy students who don't want to type their research papers.

☠ $ $ *tried it* ○

145 **CHARGE FOR ACCESS TO YOUR WIRELESS.** People are always trying to hook free wireless. But if you've got a secured system, there's no reason other people can't use it as well—provided they pay you for it. Just make sure all your files are secure; you don't want someone to pay you for hacking into your bank account.

☠ ☠ $ *tried it* ○

146 **RENT OUT YOUR COMPUTER FOR OTHERS TO RUN PRO-GRAMS ON.** Some projects need a lot of computing power. We're talking a *lot*! If you're okay with giving out access to your computer, you can rent it out just as you would any other appliance. Of course, it stays in your home and everything's done online. But you can be part of a research project—and get paid for it!

☠ $ $ *tried it* ○

147 **DATA MINE.** The amount of raw data doubles every three years. But raw data's no good unless someone analyzes it for patterns that turn it into information. If you don't mind poring over endless streams of statistics, and if you've got a head for math and algorithms, this is your chance to make money by creating info.

☠ $ $ *tried it* ○

148 **BECOME A DATA PROCESSOR.** Tapping away at endless streams of information isn't the most exciting way to spend your day, but it'll put money in your pocket. It's cubicle life at its most Dilbertesque—but what the heck! It's income.

☠ $ $ *tried it* ○

149 **BECOME A VIRTUAL ASSISTANT.** Nowadays, a busy executive needs this, that, and the other—and all in the next ten minutes. Sitting at your computer, you can meet those needs with a few keystrokes and the click of a mouse button. No need to even leave your living room. Check out opportunities online for part-time and full-time positions.

☠ $ $ *tried it* ○

Behind Your Computer

150 **SELL REPAIRED JUNK ON EBAY.** If you're Mr. Fix-It, repair stuff you don't need anymore and post it on craigslist. You'll be amazed at the things people will buy.

☠   *$ $*   *tried it* ◯

151 **HOCK YOUR CRAFTS ONLINE.** Is your house full of knitted pot holders or needlepoint pictures of kittens? Someone out there will find it valuable. Sell them on eBay and you could make more than expected.

☠   *$*   *tried it* ◯

152 **ENTER SWEEPSTAKES.** Are you waiting for Ed McMahon to show up at your door and surprise you with a fat check? Nowadays, all sorts of sweepstakes are organized in one place online, like at *www.online-sweepstakes.com.*

☠   *$ $ $*   *tried it* ◯

153 **BUILD A MYSPACE PAGE FOR A COMPANY.** MySpace is one of the most popular sites now for companies to advertise their products. Millions of people sign on everyday and word of mouth is one of the best ways to get a product out there. Offer your MySpace skills to a company.

☠ ☠   *$ $*   *tried it* ◯

154 **BUILD A FACEBOOK PAGE FOR A PRODUCT.** Just like MySpace, Facebook is another popular networking website. If you are familiar with the ins and outs of Facebook, make a page for a new product.

☠   *$ $*   *tried it* ◯

155 **SEND OUT SOCIAL NETWORK BLASTS.** Companies rely on social network blasts to get the word out about their product or service. If you're on MySpace and Facebook all day anyway, why not get paid for it? Offer to be a blaster.

☠   *$ $*   *tried it* ○

156 **ADVOCATE BUSINESSES VIA TWITTER.** If you aren't familiar with Twitter, it's a free social networking and microblogging site. Companies want average Joes to advocate their products and services. Word-of-mouth goes far, so jump online and twitter away.

☠   *$ $*   *tried it* ○

157 **HOST AN AFFILIATE PROGRAM ON YOUR WEBSITE.** Websites can be valuable property. There are plenty of businesses that would like the chance to talk to your visitors. Give them the opportunity—for a reasonable fee. And make sure you're okay with the content of the program. You don't want to piss off any regular visitors to your site.

☠   *$*   *tried it* ○

158 **LAUNCH A PODCAST.** If you know a lot about a certain topic and have dreams of being on the radio, launching a podcast is the next best thing. Talk about aliens, the state of the economy, the latest reality show phenomenon. You'll be surprised at how many people want to listen.

☠ ☠   *$ $ $*   *tried it* ○

159 **BEG ONLINE.** Just as Dustin "Screech" Diamond did when his house was going to be foreclosed, you too can beg for money online. Don't underestimate the charity of others when you need it most.

☠ ☠   *$ $ $*   *tried it* ○

Behind Your Computer

160 **CHARGE FOR ONLINE ADVICE.** You're the smartest person you know. Bet a lot of other people think so too. And they'll pay for your insights into their problems. Set up a pay website as Uncle Friendly Advisor or Auntie Knows-it-all and you're all set.

☠ $ *tried it* ○

161 **LAUNCH A SUBSCRIPTION-BASED WEBCAM.** Maybe it's you playing with your pets. Maybe it's taking visitors on a tour of your garden. Maybe it's . . . *ahem!* . . . other stuff. But people will pay to watch you. Really. You're that interesting.

☠ $ $ *tried it* ○

162 **CHARGE FOR CYBERSEX.** Sex is *everywhere* these days. Everyone's doing it, talking about it, talking about other people doing it. . . . Why not get in on the act? Play out others' sexual fantasies online, once they pay up to your PayPal account. But beware—you never *really* know who's on the other end.

☠ ☠ ☠ $ $ *tried it* ○

163 **LAUNCH A PORN SITE.** Maybe it's the Christmas Eve sex tape you and your partner made when you'd both had too much champagne. Or maybe it's the Valentine's Day photos you took. In any case, if you put them online, people will pay money to see them. Of course, you'll just have to keep supplying videos and photos. Think you can handle that?

☠ ☠ ☠ $ $ $ *tried it* ○

164 **STRIP ONLINE.** Stripping online is pretty straightforward—bust out the webcam and take it all off. But you can get creative by hosting a strip poker site, therefore doubling your earnings (assuming you win occasionally).

☠ ☠ ☠ ☠ $ $ $ *tried it* ○

165 **TAKE E-SURVEYS.** Did you know some companies will pay for your opinions? Take twenty or thirty minutes to fill out an online survey and pocket your fee. Of course, not all surveys pay, so you'll have to dig around. And have some opinions.

☠ $ *tried it* ○

166 **TRADE UP (ON EBAY).** A brilliant man named Kyle MacDonald once traded his way up eBay starting with a red paper clip, and fourteen trades later he owned a house in Saskatchewan. Check out his amazing story at *http://oneredpaperclip.blogspot.com*. If he can do it, so can you. Start with something small (like a paper clip) and see what you end up with.

☠ ☠ $ $ $ $ *tried it* ○

167 **CLICK ON ADS.** You don't even have to type. Just go to a website, click on an ad, and earn bucks. What could be simpler than that? About the biggest problem you might have is getting a sore finger from clicking so much. But watch out for scams!

☠ $ *tried it* ○

168 **CHECK OUT AMAZON'S MECHANICAL TURK.** Computers are good at lots of stuff, but not so much at others. So companies will hire you to do things computers can't. Like identify objects in a photo or transcribe an audio recording. The pay's not great, but every little bit adds up.

☠ $ *tried it* ○

Behind Your Computer

169 **ANSWER ONLINE QUESTIONS.** It's simple. Check out *www.mahalo.com/answers* and see if there are questions you know the answer to. Once you post your answer and it's confirmed, you'll be paid a dollar for each question you answer (actually, more like seventy-five cents, since PayPal has to take their chunk). Put your thinking cap on.

☠ $ *tried it* ○

170 **SUBMIT TO ASSOCIATED CONTENT.** It's sort of like writing for an online encyclopedia. You look at what content the site—which is an open source content site—is soliciting articles for and then bang away at your computer until you've got something. You always wanted to be a writer, right?

☠ $ $ *tried it* ○

171 **SELL YOUR CONTACTS TO JIGSAW.** Jigsaw, an online business directory, will pay bucks for the contents of your address files. Of course, you've got to be sure all the people you're selling are okay with being part of a public directory. But if they're cool with it, mine this vein of contact gold.

☠ ☠ $ *tried it* ○

172 **ENTER ONLINE GAME TOURNAMENTS.** If you've got a mind for games, you might be in line for some bucks. More and more games—from Monopoly to Scrabble to Magic: The Gathering—are played online. Move up the great pyramid of winners and you can collect cash prizes.

☠ $ $ $ *tried it* ○

173 **GO TO CASHCRATE.COM.** It's a way for companies to try out their products and services on you and get you to fill out surveys, questionnaires, and polls. It's a way for you to make a little extra money. Go on the site, sign up, and start clicking.

☠ $ *tried it* ○

174 **BET ON ONLINE GAMES.** Every sport needs spectators and every spectator sport needs gamblers. As online gaming becomes more popular—and more and more people start participating—see what kind of side action you can get throwing some dough down on online competitions. Gamers love to talk trash, so if you get one going good enough, you might just make some money.

☠ ☠ $ $ *tried it* ○

175 **PLAY ONLINE POKER.** C'mon! You know you've always wanted to be a riverboat gambler. Thanks to the Internet, you can play poker online for stakes as high or low as you want. Remember—the higher the risk, the higher the reward. You can even wear a silk waistcoat and gold watch chain.

☠ ☠ ☠ $ $ $ *tried it* ○

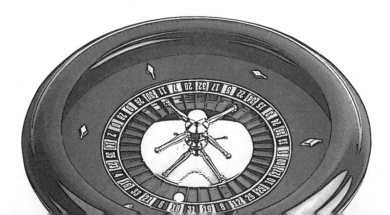

176 **PLAY FANTASY FOOTBALL.** So what if you're not six feet two and don't weight 280 pounds. You can be a five-foot-three nerd with glasses and a pocket protector and still play football. Fantasy football, that is. All you need is a good Internet connection and a head for sports statistics.

☒ $ $ *tried it* ○

177 **PLAY FANTASY BASEBALL.** Get your baseball cap on, get your computer fired up, and get online for some serious fantasy baseball action. Players pay money into a league fund and get back money based on the number of games their team wins.

☒ $ $ *tried it* ○

178 **PLAY FANTASY BASKETBALL.** It's all about knowing the game. You don't have to be good on the court; you just have to know which pro basketball players are good. Get online, get into a league, and get a team together. If you know your sports stats, you can get a good return on investment.

☒ $ $ *tried it* ○

179 **BECOME A FANTASY COMMISSIONER.** The commish supervises the trades between teams, league rules and stats, schedules, and scoring options. As commish, you can also charge a small fee per transaction for these services. Be fair, be square, and make money.

☒ $ $ *tried it* ○

CHAPTER 4

Use Your Body

Some of us have been given a chance by natural selection to use our bodies (in a variety of ways) to make money (in a variety of amounts). Now whether you were granted a beautiful body, bulging biceps, or insensitivity to pain, we don't know—but we do know you can make a buck using each.

180 **SELL YOUR BODY TO SCIENCE.** The trick here is to cash in while you're still alive. You could take part in a study for a new drug, be the guinea pig for college psych students, or be one of those people walking on treadmills with little suction cups all over them (and pray they keep the suction cups above your waist).

☠ ☠   *$ $ $*   *tried it* ○

181 **SELL YOUR PLASMA.** You probably didn't even know you had plasma. So you won't miss it, right? Plasma is the part of your blood that carries nutrients to your cells and doctors are willing to pay you for it. Check out the Yellow Pages or college campuses for the closest plasma collection center, and earn anywhere from $35 to $100—but you can only donate twice a week.

☠ ☠   *$ $*   *tried it* ○

182 **SELL YOUR HAIR.** Some generous souls actually donate their hair, but your soul isn't very generous, is it? People will pay big bucks for wigs and hair extensions, and if you have long hair, you may as well earn something for it. Visit TheHairTrader.com to find out how you can earn crazy cash for your coif (though you may have to invest in a few hats after your cut).

☠   *$ $ $*   *tried it* ○

183 **SELL YOUR SPERM.** If the idea of a kid who shares genes with you running around somewhere doesn't freak you out, then by all means, sell your baby batter to a sperm bank. While there's more to it than porking a plastic cup (you have to undergo a medical history test before you're considered), it can be fun to earn money for doing something you were going to do anyway. Talk to your doctor about where to find a reputable sperm bank (because a regular bank teller would probably slap you).

☠ ☠   *$ $*   *tried it* ○

184 **SELL YOUR EGGS.** When it comes to selling your baby-making equipment, the ladies have a tougher time than the fellas. True, egg donors are better paid than sperm salesmen (making up to 5 grand), but they must undergo hormone therapy and outpatient surgery to earn their dough. It's important to talk to your doctor about the potential risks, and to find a reputable fertility clinic to handle your donation.

☠ ☠ ☠ $ $ $ *tried it* ○

185 **BECOME A SURROGATE MOTHER.** They say your body is a temple. In this case, it's more like a vessel. Acting as a surrogate is a noble service but a physically and emotion-ally taxing experience. While profitable, this is one under-taking that you definitely shouldn't pursue for money alone. Talk to your doctor if you're interested (and fertile).

☠ ☠ ☠ $ $ $ $ *tried it* ○

186 **TAKE PART IN AN EXPERIMENTAL DRUG TRIAL.** This is a tricky one. Best-case scenario: you wind up in the placebo group and get paid to take some sugar pills. And then there's the chance you develop serious medical complica-tions due to a bad drug or interaction ("Look, Ma, I've got three nipples!"). At ClinicalCollection.com, you can sign up to receive an e-mail notice every time there is a trial in your area.

☠ ☠ ☠ ☠ $ $ $ *tried it* ○

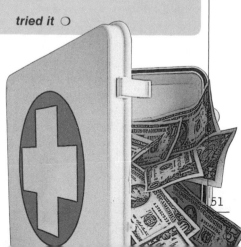

187 **PARTICIPATE IN A SMOKING CESSATION CLINIC.** Newsflash: smoking cigarettes is bad for you. With millions of people trying to kick butts, doctors are constantly researching ways to aid struggling smokers. To test the effectiveness, medical professionals pay smokers to try their method of quitting. Not only will you receive a stipend, but you'll also save money in the long run when you no longer have to shell out your hard-earned cash for a pack o' smokes.

☠   *$ $*   *tried it* ○

188 **TAKE PART IN A STRESS STUDY.** Work is usually stressful, but this is a job where you're actually supposed to get stressed—so that the guys in white lab coats can observe how stress affects the body. These can be hard to come by, so if you're interested in taking part in one of these studies, contact as many hospitals as possible to get your name on a list of potential guinea pigs.

☠   *$ $*   *tried it* ○

189 **COMPLETE A STUDY ABOUT DEPRESSION.** The bad economy is enough to make anybody feel the blues. Earn money off this misery by participating in studies run by medical companies that want to take advantage of others' sadness. The money earned should help solve your depression.

☠   *$ $*   *tried it* ○

190 **ENTER A SLEEP STUDY.** While seemingly simple, sleeping is a complex medical subject—not to mention a million-dollar industry. In order for sleep specialists to further understand the various sleep issues, they need to observe individuals in a state of sleep. While it won't be as cozy as your own bed and pillow, this is one place where it pays to be caught sleeping on the job.

☠   *$ $*   *tried it* ○

191 **BECOME A HUMAN BILLBOARD.** Admit it: part of you has always wanted a badass tattoo. Why not profit from it by inking a corporate logo or company name on yourself? In 2005, a Utah woman auctioned off her forehead on eBay for $10,000. While it screams "sell out" (not to mention desperation), it's likely you could find a company willing to do the same for you.

☠ ☠ ☠ ☠ $ $ $ $ *tried it* ○

192 **NAME YOUR KID AFTER A COMPANY.** If you're going to name your child something crazy like Chevrolet or ESPN, you may as well get paid to do it. And you can put the money you make into a savings account so the kid can go to therapy when he grows up.

☠ ☠ $ $ *tried it* ○

193 **ASSIST IN A NATURAL BIRTH.** They say childbirth is a beautiful thing. They're lying. It's a physically, emotionally, and visually challenging experience to assist a woman giving birth—especially when that woman hasn't had an epidural. It is also a rewarding job, and if you have a supportive nature (and a strong stomach), visit Midwifery Today.com to find out more about becoming a midwife, doula, or childbirth coach.

☠ ☠ $ $ *tried it* ○

194 **BECOME A CONFIDENTIAL INFORMANT.** If you're in the know about some criminal activity, consider offering your knowledge to law enforcement. While the threat of retaliation is very real if you are found out (i.e., you could get killed), it won't take up too much of your time, and you'd actually help fight crime—no cape required.

☠ ☠ ☠ ☠ $ $ *tried it* ○

Use Your Body

195 **BECOME A PRIVATE EYE.** Want to take your nosiness to a whole new level? Consider a job as a private eye. It's probably not as exciting as the movies make it look (most private investigators spend the majority of their time investigating insurance claims), but you can make some decent cash.

☠ ☠ ☠ $ $ $ *tried it* ○

196 **CREATE AND POST A VIRAL VIDEO.** This can be tough to capitalize on, but it's always fun to get together with your buddies and humiliate yourselves on camera (bonus for bodily harm!). There's always the chance that you'll become an Internet sensation, but otherwise you'll end up as broke as when you started.

☠ $ $ *tried it* ○

197 **WORK AS A PERSONAL TRAINER.** You only have to look around at the number of people shopping at Lane Bryant to realize that there are a lot of overweight and out-of-shape people out there. Every New Year, thousands of doughy Americans resolve that this will be the year they get in shape! Why not become a licensed personal trainer and help them on their way? You'll be lean and green in no time. Visit the Aerobics and Fitness Association of America at *www.afaa.com.*

☠ $ $ $ *tried it* ○

198 **BECOME A RUNNING COACH.** Admit it: driving by runners makes you feel like a lazy slob. If you can't run them over, why not join them? Act as a running coach (whose job appears to be to run along with their clients saying things like "You're doing great!" or "Keep it up!") and get paid to get in shape.

☠ $ $ *tried it* ○

199 **BE AN EXERCISE BUDDY.** Are you a motivated fitness buff but don't have the time or desire to get certified as a personal trainer? Offer your services as an exercise buddy. Paunchy people who lack your motivation will be motivated to work out more often if they know they'll face your wrath if they don't.

☠ ☠   *$ $*   ***tried it*** ○

200 **ENTER A BODYBUILDING CONTEST.** From the very first time you saw the *SNL* skit "Pumping Up with Hans and Franz," you've wanted to pump *zee* weights. You're probably already hitting up the gym to release your frustrations over your current financial crunch, so go further and compete to make money. It's time to pump *you* up, girlie man.

☠ ☠   *$ $ $*   ***tried it*** ○

201 **ENTER A BEAUTY PAGEANT.** While not a reliable source of income, working the pageant circuit can be a profitable venture. If you don't mind putting Vaseline on your teeth or being judged solely on your looks, enter a beauty pageant for a chance to win some big bucks (though you'll have to shell out for your own hideous dress and bikini for the bathing suit portion of the competition).

☠   *$ $ $*   ***tried it*** ○

202 **ENTER AN EATING CONTEST.** If one hot dog is good, fifty-nine must be fantastic, right? Maybe not if you have to eat them in twelve minutes as world record holder Joey Chestnut did in the 2008 Nathan's Hot Dog Eating Contest. If you possess some gastronomical fortitude, then enter a professional eating competition—if throwing up in front of strangers is your idea of fun.

☠ ☠ ☠   *$ $*   ***tried it*** ○

203 **ENTER A JINGLE CONTEST.** Think you have the chops to create a jingle catchy enough to stick in people's heads and send them to store shelves? Try your hand at writing jingles. Oreo once offered a $10,000 prize and a trip to New York City to the lucky person who could wow them with their musical advertisement. That can buy a lot of cream filling.

☠   *$ $ $*   *tried it* ○

204 **WORK AS A BOUNCER.** Do you have big muscles and an elevated sense of self-importance? Try a job as a doorman or bouncer at a bar or nightclub. While not as profitable as bartending, bouncers are often paid well by business owners who want to keep the riffraff out. So hit the weight room and put your muscles to a task more useful than flexing in the mirror.

☠ ☠ ☠ ☠   *$ $ $*   *tried it* ○

205 **REPO.** One job that actually becomes more secure when the economy is in the toilet is working as a repo officer. It can be a less than pleasant chore to visit those in a cash crunch and leave with their crap, but their loss is your gain, so stop worrying about other people's feelings and start taking their stuff.

☠ ☠ ☠   *$ $ $*   *tried it* ○

206 **JOIN THE CIRCUS.** Are you a bearded lady? Can you contort your body to fit into a tiny box while wearing a skintight unitard? A career in the circus may be for you. True, you'll probably spend a lot of time living in trailer and shoveling elephant shit, but you'll definitely meet some interesting characters.

☠ ☠   *$ $*   *tried it* ○

Use Your Body

207 **BECOME A STUNT MAN.** You already enjoy pulling off *Jackass*-like stunts, so why not get paid for putting your life in danger? Falling off buildings, being set on fire, and getting thrown through plate glass will replace the ho-hum of sending a fax, updating spreadsheets, and checking e-mails. Now if that's not incentive enough—what is?

☠ ☠ ☠ ☠ $ $ $ *tried it* ○

208 **WORK AS A STUNT DRIVER.** The only thing Hollywood likes more than a gratuitous boob shot is a good car chase. It's far too risky to send Will Smith off a cliff at 120 miles per hour, so movie studios hire stunt drivers for the challenge. Is it a rush? Absolutely. Will a lowly director's assistant scrape you off the pavement? Quite likely. But this testosterone-pumping job can pay big time, so grab your helmet and head to the set.

☠ ☠ ☠ ☠ $ $ $ $ *tried it* ○

209 **COMPETE IN A RODEO.** If getting your genital region smashed against a leather saddle and your head smashed in by a horse sounds like a good time to you, try competing in a rodeo. You'll earn every penny as a bucking bronco sends you sailing to your untimely death.

☠ ☠ ☠ $ $ *tried it* ○

210 **BECOME A RODEO CLOWN.** Do you love the idea of being a bullfighter but want something a bit more humiliating? Sounds like you have all the makings of a perfect rodeo clown. The prime duty of a rodeo clown is to protect the bull rider from injury, which may sound noble, but when a red nose is added to the mix, the absurdity of the situation is off the charts.

☠ ☠ ☠ ☠ $ $ $ *tried it* ○

Use Your Body

211 **ENLIST IN THE NATIONAL GUARD.** The only thing you love more than your country? Making bank. While there is the pesky matter of basic training, enlisting in the National Guard can secure you $20,000 as well as college tuition. Plus you can actually gain some invaluable career experience, helping you get better (i.e., better paying) jobs in the future. Find out more at *www.ngb.army.mil.*

☠ ☠ ☠ ☠ $ $ $ *tried it* ○

212 **WORK AS A SECURITY GUARD.** True, society tends to mock these not-quite-police-officers, but working as a security guard can be an ideal moonlighting gig, as businesses often want someone to work security after hours. Just be sure not to fall off your Segway.

☠ ☠ ☠ $ $ *tried it* ○

213 **WORK AS A BODYGUARD.** Hey, if Kevin Costner did it, you can too. If you know someone rich, famous, or powerful enough to need a bodyguard, put your brawn to use and work as a bodyguard. Then again, if you know someone rich, famous, or powerful, what do you need this book for?

☠ ☠ ☠ $ $ $ *tried it* ○

214 **HIRE OUT AS A MERCENARY.** Are you looking to turn your military experience into more money? Sell yourself to the highest bidder and join a war you have no interest in, except for your personal investment. Be careful though. If you follow through with this idea, you'll become a real-life Rambo—without the advantage of a Hollywood ending.

☠ ☠ ☠ ☠ $ $ $ $ *tried it* ○

Use Your Body

215 **ENTER A STREET FIGHT.** Ever since *Fight Club* came out in 1999, many a dude thinks he can be a legendary street fighter. Why not challenge this dude (that's *you*)? If you're built more like Tom Thumb than Tom Brady, be sure to seek out a challenger you'll be able to handle.

☠ ☠ ☠ ☠ $ *tried it* ○

216 **TEACH A SELF-DEFENSE CLASS.** The world is F'd up sometimes, and people—especially women—need to be able to protect themselves from creeps. If you are a trained fighter, teach a self-defense class. If you can get enough students to sign up, you can earn a fistful of dollars—just make sure your students don't use their new knowledge on you.

☠ ☠ $ $ $ *tried it* ○

217 **RUN A KICK-BOXING CLASS.** Any venture where you can work your aggression out while making money is a good one. And the fact that members of the opposite sex will be following your every move while sweating and panting is just a bonus. Find out how to become a certified kickboxing instructor at the Aerobics and Fitness Association of America's website, *www.afaa.com.*

☠ ☠ $ *tried it* ○

218 **LEAD A BOXING CLASS.** No longer the brute sport that you're embarrassed to admit you follow (that's the UFC), boxing is now a popular fitness activity. If you're an avid boxer, consider making your hobby your livelihood by getting certified and working as a boxing instructor. Visit *www.afaa.com.*

☠ ☠ $ *tried it* ○

219 **SPIN AWAY.** Spinning is one of the fastest-growing aerobic activities due to the effectiveness and efficiency of the work out. If you're motivated to ride a bike without going anywhere while yelling at a room full of strangers, visit AFAA .com—and don't forget your bike shorts.

☠ $ $ *tried it* ○

220 **WIN A ROAD RACE.** If you're a runner, try to put your healthy habit to further use by entering a road race. While big races like the Boston Marathon can get you thousands of dollars, you'll likely only receive a small cash prize when entering local races. If you win a few times, though, you'll have enough money to buy yourself some new running sneakers to replace your worn-out pair.

☠ $ *tried it* ○

221 **RUN A SPORTS CLINIC.** Were you a baseball hero in high school? Have you successfully taught all seven of your nieces to ride a bike without training wheels? Put your skills to use as a sports clinic instructor. Time-taxed moms and dads will be happy to shell out a few bucks so they don't have to teach their kids how to hit a fastball.

☠ $ $ *tried it* ○

222 **TAKE A PUNCH FOR MONEY.** Every once in awhile, a dude wants to punch another dude in the face. However, the general public and law usually frown upon this intelligent hobby. Why not give someone permission to punch you in the face for a fee? For a better chance at getting someone to take you up on the offer, try at a testosterone-charged place like a gym or a bar during a football game.

☠ ☠ ☠ $ *tried it* ○

Use Your Body

223 **BET ON ROCK, PAPER, SCISSORS.** Parlay your ability to predict what others will throw out in order to make some money—and show your friends how inferior they are. Don't get too cocky, though. The last thing you want to do is go up on a friend and then have a few miscued scissors cut your winnings down to nothing.

☠ $ *tried it* ○

224 **CALL HEADS OR TAILS FOR CASH.** Even if you don't *figuratively* have two nickels to rub together, chances are you have a coin in your pocket. Just be sure you have some money to back up your mouth; otherwise *your* head will be rolling. And if your opponent lacks listening comprehension skills, use the Ralph Kramden method: say, "Heads I win and tails you lose."

☠ $ *tried it* ○

225 **ODDS, EVENS, *SHOOT!*** Decide who takes odds and who takes evens, stick your hand behind your back, and on the call of *shoot*, send out one or two fingers in unison with your opponent—fingers crossed that the final digit count adds up to the side you've selected.

☠ $ *tried it* ○

226 **PLAY MERCY FOR MONEY.** Does the debt over your head send you into Hulk-like rages? Good. Use this to your advantage and bet on your strength. However, know when to call it quits. You can't claim disability if you broke your fingers in a back alley game of mercy.

☠ ☠ $ *tried it* ○

Use Your Body

227 **CASH IN ON RIDICULOUS DARES.** That little kid in *A Christmas Story* stuck his tongue to a frozen pole and he didn't even get paid. Next time you're at a bar (because these situations work best when there is alcohol involved), approach the tipsiest guy or girl in the place and bet them however much that you won't _____. Odds are, someone is drunk enough to take you up on it.

☠ ☠ $ *tried it* ○

228 **GIVE GOLF LESSONS.** Golf may be a gentleman's game, but there are plenty of idiots out there looking to learn how to hit the links without looking like a moron. If you can swing the sticks decently, give lessons to Tiger wannabes and be sure to capitalize on the expense of the sport. You can advertise your services at public courses or in the pro shops of private clubs. If they'll pay a hundred dollars for one round or two hundred dollars for a pair of pink pants with whales on them, surely golfers will pay a goodly amount for individual lessons.

☠ $ $ *tried it* ○

229 **WAIT ON TABLES.** The general public will test your patience when you're slinging drinks and burgers. However, depending on the size, location, and type of restaurant, this profession can get you cash quickly. Better practice your fake smile.

☠ $ $ *tried it* ○

230 **SELL YOUR SOUL.** Faust did it. So did Bart Simpson and Dorian Gray. If you're desperate enough, pawn your existence off to an interested party. Be warned, though: eternity is a wicked long time. Throw it up on eBay and see what you can get for eternal damnation.

☠ ☠ ☠ ☠ $ $ $ $ *tried it* ○

231 **SET OUT AS A TELEGRAM SINGER.** You sing to people on the street when you're drunk, so delivering a singing telegram isn't too different except you're sober (potentially). Start a service where people can request you to tunefully deliver any message. Then go out there and shine (bottle of tequila in hand, optional).

☠ $ $ *tried it* ○

232 **MODEL FOR AN ART CLASS.** If the only time you sit still for a long period of time involves the sports section and a courtesy flush, this job may not be for you. Art classes often need live models, and it doesn't involve much more than sitting (or standing) around while strangers stare at you and attempt to recreate your likeness. Boring? Yes. Easier than brick laying? Hell yeah.

☠ $ *tried it* ○

233 **BE A NUDE MODEL FOR AN ART CLASS.** Here is where you need some, ahem, balls to succeed. While it's uncomfortable to be nude in front of strangers, art students view their models as part of the artistic process, which they take very seriously. So cast your fears aside (as well as your undies), and contact the art departments at local community centers and colleges to see if they need nude models.

☠ ☠ $ $ *tried it* ○

234 **POSE NUDE FOR A MAGAZINE.** Next time you're at the gas station, count how many adult magazines there are behind the counter. They have to fill the pages, right? While getting professional pictures taken will set you back, it doesn't take anything but guts to ask a friend or your partner to take a shot of you in the buff and send it off to a number of adult magazines. If they decide they want you to model, you can earn thousands of dollars a day—and guarantee your place in gas stations everywhere.

☠ ☠ ☠ $ $ $ $ *tried it* ○

Use Your Body

235 **BECOME A BELLY DANCER.** Admit it: you break it down Bollywood style when no one is watching. What's the big deal? You'll have a veil over your face anyway. Post ads for your hip-shaking service online, and earn some cash while you entertain.

☠ $ $ *tried it* ○

236 **GO-GO DANCE.** If you have a sense of rhythm and like to attract attention, consider working in a nightclub as a go-go dancer. These days, it's less about go-go boots than it is booty shorts, but this gig can be a fun way to shake your ass and make some cash.

☠ ☠ $ $ *tried it* ○

237 **STRIP.** Whether it's your second job or amateur night at a strip club, if you have a decent-ish body, you can find someone who will pay to watch you dance naked. So grab your booby tassels and head out to The Lust Lounge and see if they need any strippers.

☠ ☠ ☠ $ $ *tried it* ○

238 **BE AN ESCORT.** We're not talking the type of escort that Charlie Sheen enjoys so much. If you're a social and attractive person, someone may be interested in hiring you to be a companion, a date to a special event, or a self-esteem booster. Escorts can earn up to a hundred dollars an hour so if you would be comfortable being someone's date for hire, hit the Net and find a service that hires escorts—without expecting them to sleep with their clients.

☠ ☠ ☠ ☠ $ $ $ $ *tried it* ○

239 **HUSTLE POOL.** Do your best Fast Eddie from *The Hustler* and make some money at the pool halls. Start out with younger, more inexperienced players (but make sure they're not hustling you) then move on to bigger bets with better players. Just make sure you don't get called out as hustler—or else it'll be a cue stick to your corner pocket.

☠ ☠ ☠ $ $ $ *tried it* ○

240 **HUSTLE PICK-UP BASKETBALL GAMES.** You may not be LeBron James, but if you can pull off the *White Men Can't Jump* angle, it'll be a financial *swish*. Beforehand, study the skill level of the players on the court. Lose at first then take it to the basket when you raise the stakes.

☠ ☠ ☠ $ $ *tried it* ○

241 **BE A CARDSHARK.** Whether it's just scamming friends into buying into "beginner's luck," or taking it up a few notches to *Rounders*-style play, you can definitely bring in the chips by playing it slick on the felt. Just be careful who you're playing with—you never know when your luck will run out, and you'll end up with your teeth knocked out.

☠ ☠ $ $ $ *tried it* ○

Use Your Body

242 **REFEREE.** Sick of yelling about how blind that zebra is when you're watching the game on TV? Well, put your money where your mouth is and show off your officiating skills by reffing local basketball, football, or soccer games. Watch out though, you're not the only armchair authority—and soccer moms are known to bite.

☠ ☠ $ $ *tried it* ○

243 **UMP.** You've obsessed over the strike zone for years. Now it's time to put your obsession to use and make a profit. Become an umpire in an amateur or little league, and cash in while calling strikes. Make sure you kick out those parents and managers who give you any guff.

☠ $ $ *tried it* ○

244 **RUN THE SCOREBOARD.** You're keeping track of the score anyway—and the fouls, errors, and time. Why not get a side job running the show? Go to your local high school and offer your services. You better be accurate though. There's likely enough creatine in some of those kids that an error on your part could lead to a foul ball in your face.

☠ ☠ $ *tried it* ○

245 **HOLD A BEARD-OFF.** Think you can grow the sickest stache? Get a group of buddies together and bet on who can grow the longest, bushiest, gnarliest beard. Set an end date and let the growing begin. You can bet on yourself or on your hairiest friends. But remember, just because someone has a full mop on top doesn't mean he can grow anything a fifteen-year-old boy couldn't.

☠ $ $ *tried it* ○

246 **SCARE UP SOME SCRATCH BY SCARING FOR OTHERS.** When people have been wronged, they often wish they could take revenge on friend and foe alike with a good fright—something that could cause a little leak in the offending person's pants. That's where you come in. You've seen enough horror movies that you could scare the crap out of Wes Craven himself. Charge to set up scares— just be certain you can deliver and won't embarrass your subscriber even more.

☠ ☠ $ $ *tried it* ○

247 **PUNK FOR PAY.** Ashton Kutcher may be a bit of a jackass, but his show *Punked* was a pop culture phenomenon. Most of us would love to pull a prank on someone in our life but fear the consequences. Since your buddy doesn't have the balls to e-mail the photo of his boss passed out at the Christmas party to the entire company, offer to do it for him—for a fee. After all, what's it to you?

☠ ☠ ☠ $ $ *tried it* ○

Use Your Body

CHAPTER 5

Charge Lazy People

Remember in Chapter 2 when we told you to get off your ass? Well, let's hope everyone hasn't bought this book and taken our advice. (Actually, *we* hope everyone has, but for your sake we won't keep our fingers crossed.) That's because you can cash in on others' choices to hire out. You wouldn't believe what some people pay for—go out and make some loot from your lazy friends.

248 **MAKE WAKE UP CALLS.** Why would people ever pay you to call them when they could just buy an alarm clock? Because they're idiots. So capitalize on their idiocy by offering your services as a wake-up caller. Just think of how fun it will be to create your own signature wake-up greeting. You're being paid to irritate people—what's more fun than that?

☠ $ *tried it* ○

249 **DO OTHER PEOPLE'S CHORES FOR CASH.** No one likes doing chores—but some people actually hate it enough to pay you to do it for them. Throw an ad on craigslist, post a flyer at a college hangout, or offer your services through word of mouth. Before you know it, you'll be folding someone else's laundry. Sweet victory!

☠ $ *tried it* ○

250 **CLEAN OUT OTHERS' CELLARS.** After you've swept up their basement, cleaned up the cobwebs, and hauled out all types of trash, ask if you can keep a few "pieces of junk" that you found. They'll most likely agree—*why would anything of value be in the basement?*—and you'll be the owner of the long-lost missing footage from *The Lady from Shanghai.* Shame on them for not knowing what they had.

☠ $ $ *tried it* ○

251 **TIDY UP ATTICS.** The up-upstairs can get kind of gross with all sorts of dust and debris, not to mention possible rodent infestation. So you better pack some protective gear when you go to make your clean sweep. Just pray the corpse of the owner's rejected twin isn't rotting away up there. That's one mess you probably don't want to handle.

☠ ☠ $ $ *tried it* ○

Charge Lazy People

252 **CLEAN OUT A BARN.** It's a lot like cleaning a garage, but more charming and rustic. And usually barns are a lot bigger than garages or sheds so there's even more room for crap to pile up. So the next time you see a big ol' barn, offer to clean it for the owner. Maybe you'll actually find something worth keeping.

☠ ☠ $ $ *tried it* ○

253 **CLEAN OUT SOMEONE ELSE'S GARAGE.** Cleaning out your garage sucks. You feel like you want to throw stuff out and start fresh, but you struggle with the idea of parting with your lunchbox collection. You have no qualms about throwing out other people's precious memories though. So offer to do someone else's unpleasant chore—for pay. It will still suck, but afterward you'll have enough money to buy yourself a beer to drown your sorrows.

☠ $ *tried it* ○

254 **WORK AS A CHAUFFEUR.** If you live in a city where many people don't have cars or where the public transportation system is less than ideal, use your car for cash. Depending on your route, you could even have a few jobs a day. Create free business cards online (visit VistaPrint.com) and leave them all over the place.

☠ $ $ *tried it* ○

255 **BE A DESIGNATED DRIVER.** Drunk people *hate* waiting for taxis. And drunk people are quick to part with their cash in the name of convenience. Start a DD service—in addition to getting paid maybe you'll even get flowers sent to you, as some liquor ads would have you believe.

☠ ☠ $ $ *tried it* ○

256 **WASH CARS.** Automatic car washers never get cars to that factory shine. But a hand wash and wax will get even the dumpiest ride looking like it's still got a few miles left in it. Canvass your neighborhood (focusing on people who are unable to wash their own cars) and offer to wash their wheels. You'll get the satisfaction of having a nice clean car—even though it's not yours.

☠ $ *tried it* ○

257 **MOW LAWNS.** True, most people who mow lawns for pay usually haven't hit puberty. But those whippersnappers have nothing on you. Advertise your services online through craigslist or your local newspaper and enjoy a throwback to your youth while you're pushing the mower in the sun.

☠ $ *tried it* ○

258 **RAKE LEAVES.** The backaches. The blisters. *Ahh*, fall! Create fliers advertising your raking skills and post them at senior and community centers. Pretty soon you'll be so busy your back will spasm and your fingers will bleed—but you'll be able to afford ice packs and bandages.

☠ ☠ $ *tried it* ○

259 **SHOVEL SNOW.** Another season, another crappy chore that no one wants to do. People are more than willing to shell out cash rather than spend hours in the snow doing backbreaking work. Next time the snow starts, bring your shovel to a densely populated neighborhood and start knocking on doors. You'll be waist deep in no time.

☠ ☠ $ *tried it* ○

260 **CHOP FIREWOOD.** Home-heating costs are through the roof, and more people are using fireplaces and wood-burning stoves to keep their houses toasty. The wood splitting required is tough work, so why not pay you to do it for them? This work can be physically difficult, so be careful what you axe for.

☠ ☠ $ *tried it* ○

261 **SHAPE SHRUBBERY.** Homeowners nowadays are too depressed to even look at their surrounding shrubbery, much less trim it. Take advantage of these lazy emotions and offer your services for a fee. Plus, you will be able to do an *Edward Scissorhands'* impression and shape some plants into elaborate designs.

☠ ☠ $ $ *tried it* ○

262 **TRIM TREES.** It might seem like an easy and practical thing, but people often overlook it. And before they can say *sumac*, lengthy branches are shading their backyard and overhanging their neighbor's property. If you're handy with a saw and aren't afraid of heights, hire out as a tree trimmer. After you've lopped off the limbs, offer to dispose of them for an additional fee.

☠ ☠ ☠ $ $ *tried it* ○

263 **PLANT FLOWERS.** Flowers will brighten anyone's day. Not having to worry about breaking a nail from planting those flowers will also make several people's day (mostly women of a certain age and class). Extra points for wearing short shorts for all that quality bending-over time.

☠ $ $ *tried it* ○

264 TEND A GARDEN. People are still all about the green movement, but are too busy to make that extra effort. This is where you come in and charge to take care of their garden. You can steal some of the vegetables and sell them in a farmer's market.

☠ $ *tried it* ○

265 PICK UP DOG POOP. Yes, the actual owners of the dogs are supposed to do this, but we're talking about the same people who dress their dogs in clothes, so logic is lost here. If you can find a group of people sick enough of stepping in dog mess to cough up some cash, you can turn shit into gold by cleaning neighborhoods of dog dumps. You've arrived, my friend.

☠ $ *tried it* ○

266 CLEAN FISH TANKS. Cleaning fish tanks isn't too hard (unless you've got a bunch of rogue fish à la *Finding Nemo*), but it can be a hassle. Make sure you know about the fish's habitat before you refill a salt water tank with filtered water—and never, under any circumstances, use a pretreated sponge to clean the inside of a fish tank. That's just silly.

☠ $ $ *tried it* ○

267 TRAIN OTHER PEOPLE'S PETS. Getting a new puppy or kitten can create enough of a mess (usually on furniture or the carpet) that people turn to professionals for help in training their animals. So brush up on your training skills (TheDogWhispererDVD.com is a good place to start) and become a puppy professor or a cat connoisseur—just get your pooper-scooper ready.

☠ $ $ *tried it* ○

268 **GROCERY SHOP FOR OTHER PEOPLE.** Food shopping is an annoying chore and one you may be able to turn into a moneymaking scheme. Try targeting lazy bachelors and harried housewives who dislike the task enough to pay someone else to do it for them. Make the best use of your time by doing your own shopping at the same time—just be sure you don't end up with your client's prune juice with extra fiber. You'll both be sorry.

☠   **$**   *tried it* ○

269 **DELIVER NONDELIVERY TAKE OUT.** Some of the best restaurant food is take-out only. If you live in a college town, you could make a few bucks by picking up food from restaurants and delivering it to apartments or dorms. Advertise in the college newspaper or website and your business will be booming in no time.

☠   **$ $**   *tried it* ○

270 **BE A GO-FOR.** Some people are too busy thinking about how important they are to leave the office to deliver documents or work materials. Hang fliers in the lobbies of office parks and stop by career fairs to make your services known.

☠   **$**   *tried it* ○

271 **BE AN ERRAND BOY OR GIRL.** Remember on *Seinfeld* when Elaine was Mr. Pitt's personal assistant? Her daily challenges included tasks like buying her boss socks. Create an advertisement touting your skills as a personal assistant and advertise it in the newspaper of a town with a good-sized upper class. Here's the secret: a personal assistant is just a fancy term for "errand boy." If you can stomach completing demeaning tasks, this is all you.

☠ ☠   **$ $**   *tried it* ○

Charge Lazy People

272 **HIRE YOURSELF OUT AS A MOVER.** Eventually, people with trucks will get sick enough of moving their friends' crap to say no. When that happens, the desperate and displaced can pay you to help them move. Be warned, though—you can't bitch to your paying clients like you would to your friends.

☠ $ $ *tried it* ○

273 **START YOUR OWN LAUNDRY SERVICE.** Hang up fliers in the local Laundromat advertising your services as a washer, dryer, and folder. You can schedule lots of jobs at the same time, people can drop off their laundry for you to take care of, and they're free to run errands while you take care of their clothes. Just be sure to turn down the work if someone particularly smelly or messy tries to hire you—no money is worth that.

☠ $ *tried it* ○

274 **DO OTHER PEOPLE'S IRONING.** Ironing clothes well is a test of skill and patience. If people aren't careful, they can end up with lots of clothes with iron-shaped burn marks on them. If you're a skilled ironworker, capitalize on this valuable skill by taking lazy people's money for this service. Be sure to have a disclaimer so you don't end up paying for any damaged clothes. Even the mighty have mishaps when it comes to ironing.

☠ ☠ $ *tried it* ○

275 **CLEAN THE OUTSIDES OF WINDOWS.** The risk factor for this one goes up substantially based on the height of the windows that you're cleaning. If you're standing on the ground, the risk level is around .01. But hang from the top of a thirty-story building and you've got yourself a solid 4 on the risk factor. Logically, the money also increases with height.

☠ ☠ ☠ ☠ $ $ $ *tried it* ○

276 **WORK AS A HOUSEKEEPER.** While most of us manage to keep our houses moderately clean and neat, there are people who consider housekeeping a chore beneath them. Use their snobbery to your advantage. With little initial investment (think cleaning supplies), you can start a lucrative housekeeping business. Whether or not you wear the French maid outfit is up to you.

☠ $ $ *tried it* ○

277 **START AN ENVIRONMENTALLY FRIENDLY HOUSECLEANING SERVICE.** It's never been cooler to be green. But Kermit was right—it's not easy, nor is it cheap. By using environmentally responsible cleaning supplies, you can save the environment and charge more for your services. Keep your costs down by making your own cleaning supplies from ingredients such as baking powder, vinegar, lemon, and cornstarch. Visit EarthEasy.com to learn about earth-friendly cleaning.

☠ $ $ *tried it* ○

278 **CHARGE FOR A SPRING-CLEANING SERVICE.** There's cleaning and then there's *spring cleaning*. If you want to make some extra money, make this a nude spring-cleaning service. It's a good deal!

☠ ☠ $ $ $ *tried it* ○

279 **CLEAN CARPETS.** There are some spills that a normal vacuum is just not equipped to clean. Buy a nice wet-vac and then rent out your services to the neighborhood. This is especially good for parents of small children who create messes 24/7.

☠ $ *tried it* ○

280 **CLEAN BATHROOMS.** Even people who like to clean don't usually like to clean bathrooms. If you advertise yourself as solely a bathroom cleaner you may get more customers than you'd expect since you'll be focusing on a room that people won't mind paying to have cleaned.

☠ ☠ $ $ *tried it* ○

281 **ORGANIZE OTHERS' CLOSETS.** It can be hard to face a closet full of crap. Somehow, though, it's easier when it's not your own crap that you're faced with. When you're organizing if you find "junk," suggest to the owner that you sell it for them on eBay (see entry 150)—and take a cut of course.

☠ $ $ *tried it* ○

282 **PUT IN AIR-CONDITIONING UNITS.** Is there anything more unpleasant than installing AC units in the oppressive heat? Probably not, so charge the hell out of other people and do it for them. Advertise your services in the lobbies of apartment buildings, where it's unlikely residents have central air.

☠ $ *tried it* ○

283 **TAKE OUT AIR-CONDITIONING UNITS.** For people who labored with putting the units in three months ago and cursed everything and everyone in their life during the process, you're there. Be the guy (or girl) to remove the AC unit come autumn and put it back into storage. You might be able to set up an installation gig for the end of spring—as long as you don't drop the unit out the window while removing it.

☠ $ *tried it* ○

Charge Lazy People

284 **HANG PAINTINGS.** Some people just cannot get a painting to hang straight, no matter how many times they hold the level up and step back and look at it. And finding studs in the wall? Forget about it. Help the unhandy by hanging paintings (and by help I mean charge for the service).

☠ $ *tried it* ○

285 **PATCH A DRIVEWAY.** Potholes are hard on cars. Paying a professional service to patch them is hard on the wallet. Take out the middleman by offering your patching services directly to the customer. It's not hard to figure out who might be in need; just take a stroll around your neighborhood and keep your eyes on the prize holes.

☠ ☠ $ $ *tried it* ○

286 **ACT AS A BILL PAYER.** Have you ever heard a friend complaining about the number of late fees they get from overdue bills and thought, "It's not that hard to keep track of when they're due!" Well now you can put that irritation to good use and become a professional bill payer. The money saved in late fees will go right into your pocket.

☠ $ $ *tried it* ○

287 **MAKE DUMP RUNS.** Some cities and towns don't have trash pickup, so people are forced to bring their refuse to the dump. You can see how this might be unpleasant for certain people, so take a load off of them and get paid to run to the dump.

☠ ☠ $ $ *tried it* ○

288 **RETURN GOODS.** There's just about nothing worse than waiting in line at a store to return something, but it's one of those things in life that you just can't avoid—until now! Check out the stores that have the longest, most ulcer-inducing lines and start hawking yourself as a professional returner.

☠ $ $ *tried it* ○

289 **WRITE COMPLAINT LETTERS FOR OTHERS.** There are complaint letters that sound like crazy ranting and then there are complaint letters that get the wronged party free shit. Help people out by composing well-written thought-provoking complaint letters in a way that will have the accused party apologizing profusely and offering to make it up to them.

☠ $ *tried it* ○

290 **CREATE SCRAPBOOKS FOR OTHER PEOPLE.** Scrapbooking is easy—being good at scrapbooking? Ain't so much. If you're artistically inclined, offer to put other people's pictures and mementos in a scrapbook for them. They make a great gift—and one you can get away with charging a few bucks for. Check out MemoryMakersMagazine.com for ideas and materials.

☠ $ $ *tried it* ○

291 **CREATE SOMEONE ELSE'S VISION BOARD.** Ever since *The Secret* became *The Da Vinci Code* of 2006, everyone and their mother thinks the Law of Attraction will bring them wealth, health, and happiness. But it' so much damn work! Cash in on the laziness of these not-so-visionary people and create the vision board designed to ensure that their goals and dreams become reality. True, you doing their vision board for them defeats the purpose, but they don't have to know that.

☠ ☠ $ $ *tried it* ○

Charge Lazy People

292 **WAIT IN LINE FOR OTHERS.** Whether it's camping out for tickets to a Phish reunion or standing for hours in line at the Vatican, people don't want to have to spend their precious time waiting. Grab your iPod and a good book and you can make money while waiting. Maybe you can even make enough to buy yourself a pair of those coveted tix when you get to the front of the line.

☠   *$ $*   *tried it* ○

293 **CAMP OUT FOR CONCERT TICKETS.** Camping out for concert tickets can easily escalate into an episode of *Candid Camera*—okay, maybe that's only if your name is Zack Morris and you frequently get saved by a bell. But it can still be fun. Bring a deck of cards and make some extra cash by starting an all night poker game or have a "who will fall asleep first" contests.

☠ ☠   *$ $*   *tried it* ○

294 **CLEAN POOLS.** You've seen enough movies to know what role the pool boy plays. Fulfill that fantasy by throwing on a speedo and grabbing a pole—with a net that is. You can get a great tan and meet a lot of interesting pool owners.

☠   *$*   *tried it* ○

295 **OPEN OTHERS' POOLS.** For once-a-year fast cash, open people's pools at the start of the season. This is especially lucrative if you live near a resort area so you can have the pools open by the time the happy family arrives at the beginning of the summer.

☠   *$*   *tried it* ○

296 **CLOSE OTHERS' POOLS.** Open the pools, close the pools. Same fast cash once a year, just a bit more chilly. If the pool is at a vacation home and the owners take off early, throw a pool party (or two) for some bonus dough.

☠   *$*   *tried it* ○

297 **POLISH OTHERS' SILVER.** Polishing silver may sound easy, but it's actually quite tedious and needs to be done two to six times a year to keep silver looking shiny and new. Advertise yourself to people who have recently celebrated their 25th wedding anniversary—that's the year that silver is generally the gift.

☠ $ $ *tried it* ○

298 **TAKE OUT A NEIGHBOR'S TRASH.** Maybe you did this for free when you were a kid as a good deed for an elderly neighbor. But now you're grown and good deeds don't pay the bills. Pick a neighborhood that has an early morning trash pickup or some other inconvenience that causes people to grumble about taking out the trash.

☠ $ *tried it* ○

299 **DECORATE FOR PEOPLE'S PARTIES.** Do you love throwing parties but don't have the space or resources? Use other people's money and house to throw the party of your—well, their—dreams. Get in good with the hostess and maybe she'll invite you back for subsequent parties.

☠ $ $ *tried it* ○

300 **CLEAN UP AFTER PEOPLE'S PARTIES.** If you decorate for the party and clean up after the party, it only makes sense for you to *attend* the party, right? You can try making a case for it, or you can go home and wait while everybody else has fun making a mess.

☠ ☠ $ $ *tried it* ○

301 **HELP PEOPLE GO PAPERLESS.** Green is so hot right now. There are people out there who want to go green, but just don't know how. You can help by setting them up with online billing, e-mail messages with that little "don't print this!" symbol, and reading a newspaper online.

☠ $ *tried it* ○

302 **ASSEMBLE FURNITURE.** Furniture is always making false promises. "Easy to assemble!" "No tools needed!" "Only takes ten minutes!" Forty-five minutes later and with nothing that looks like it did in the store, people need someone to call to come pick up the pieces. They need you.

☠ ☠ $ $ *tried it* ○

303 **ASSEMBLE TOYS.** There's getting paid to assemble toys for people in your community, and then there's getting scammed on the Internet by companies promising to pay you to work from home assembling toys. Make sure you're doing the legal, profitable version.

☠ $ $ *tried it* ○

304 **CARVE PUMPKINS.** You probably won't find many people who will pay for a triangle-eyed jack-o'-lantern. But if you've got mad knife skills and a good dose of artistic talent, try your hand at the fine art of pumpkin sculpture.

☠ ☠ $ *tried it* ○

305 **DO SOMEONE'S HALLOWEEN MAKEUP.** Are you skilled with a makeup brush? Put that talent to good use once a year by doing Halloween makeup. This doesn't just have to be kid's faces either. Find a group of guys dressing as pregnant cheerleaders and whip out your sluttiest lipstick.

☠ ☠ $ *tried it* ○

306 **TAKE KIDS TRICK-OR-TREATING.** You miss trick-or-treating, don't you? Try convincing your friends that their kids would score better candy if they were with you (since you're such a sweet talker). Your friends know that they'll be profiting in the long run since half their kids' take goes to them.

☠ $ *tried it* ○

307 **DECORATE OTHERS' HOME INTERIORS FOR THE HOLIDAYS.** "The stockings were hung by the chimney with care." And who do you think hung those stockings with such care? Why, the person paid to decorate the house for the holidays of course!

☠ $ $ *tried it* ○

308 **DECORATE OTHERS' HOME EXTERIORS FOR THE HOLIDAYS.** It's likely that anyone who's seen *National Lampoon's Christmas Vacation* more than once is terrified of putting up Christmas lights. Make someone the envy of all their neighbors by lighting them up from top to bottom. Just try not to fall off the roof.

☠ ☠ ☠ $ $ *tried it* ○

309 **ADDRESS AND SEAL INVITATIONS.** Extremely popular people can't be bothered to actually take part in the mundane task of addressing and sealing invites to the year's hottest bash that they're throwing. Whip out your nicest ballpoint, stock up on self-sealing envelopes, and you'll have it made.

☠ $ *tried it* ○

Charge Lazy People

310 **WRAP OTHER PEOPLE'S GIFTS.** At Christmastime people get busy—and lazy. Make sure these busy/lazy people are also rich before approaching them about your present-wrapping services. Throw on some fancy ribbon and charge extra for the style.

☠   **$**   *tried it* ○

311 **SEND OUT HOLIDAY CARDS.** The holidays are a time for being with family, celebrating the season, and spending lots and lots of money. For some extra cash, offer to send out holiday cards. Charge extra for things like calligraphy and personalized messages.

☠   **$**   *tried it* ○

312 **REMEMBER BIRTHDAYS AND SEND OUT CARDS.** Expectations run high on birthdays. So high that people are willing to pay not to have to remember them. Make sure to remind your client what was purchased for his or her loved ones so that no confusion occurs.

☠   **$ $**   *tried it* ○

313 **REMEMBER ANNIVERSARIES AND SEND GIFTS.** Outsourcing is hot these days, and it doesn't have to be out of the country. Once someone realizes that they can pay other people to handle different aspects of their life, it's hard to stop. Take advantage of this by keeping track of anniversaries for someone and sending out gifts.

☠   **$ $**   *tried it* ○

Charge Lazy People

CHAPTER 6

Be a Star

With the advent of the Internet and reality television, just about anyone can be a "star" nowadays. However, you can legitimize your celebrity by actually contributing to the artistic community. Unless, of course, your idea of an artistic contribution is to star in an online reality show.

314 **GO ON A GAME SHOW.** If you're planning a trip to the Los Angeles area, you can enter to strike it big on a game show. The downside is that you may not get on the show (and if you do, you'll be forced to fist-pump Howie Mandel or tell a witty story in three seconds to Alex Trebek) but you may be selected and win big. Visit your favorite game show's website for details on how to become lucky contestant number three.

☠ $ $ $ *tried it* ○

315 **APPLY FOR THE GENIUS GRANT.** Are you wicked smart? Prove it. Apply for a MacArthur Fellowship and you could get $500,000 in "no-strings support" from The John D. and Catherine T. MacArthur Foundation. Visit *www.macfound .org* to find out if you qualify and to apply.

☠ $ $ $ $ *tried it* ○

316 **TRY OUT FOR A REALITY SHOW.** Desperate enough to humiliate yourself on national television? Audition to join the cast of a reality show. You can drink to excess, have your sex life broadcast to millions in that creepy night-vision green, and fight with other cast members without repercussions. Some pay, some don't, but the ones that don't will at the very least get you a paid trip to where the show is filmed, or possibly a six-month rent-free stay in a crazy house like the reality-TV host monkey, MTV's *The Real World*.

☠ ☠ ☠ $ $ *tried it* ○

317 **SHOOT YOUR OWN YOUTUBE PILOT.** These days, YouTube allows you to do more than just watch a clip of Two Girls, One Cup. Series like LonelyGirl15, whose first "webisode" premiered in 2006, have caught the attention of millions and have inspired TV spin-off series internationally. So gather some friends, grab a camera, and film your pilot. At the very least, you'll be a celebrity in your own mind.

☠ $ $ *tried it* ○

318 **MAKE A DOCUMENTARY.** Actual and pseudo-intellectuals alike enjoy documentaries—whether they're about cute but endangered penguins or the problems of the American medical industry. If you can find financial backers, pick the issue du jour and film a "docu." You could end up being that Oscar winner who provides a much-needed bathroom break for those watching at home.

☠️ $ $ $ *tried it* ○

319 **SHOOT SOMEONE ELSE'S DOCUMENTARY.** Like a lot of things, a person may have a great idea, but no means (or ambition) to follow through. That's where you step in. Know how to get a great shot? Skilled at the editing process? Able to sync up audio or dub it over video? Then hire yourself out as freelance documentarian. Check out filmmaker society sites, or their group pages on Facebook. Oftentimes, people will post looking to team up with others who have different skills.

☠️ $ $ *tried it* ○

320 **FORM A BAR BAND.** Do you sing or play an instrument? Enjoy hitting the bars at night? Combine your two hobbies and form a band that plays in nightclubs and bars. While you'll never win a Grammy, you'll drink for free and get a cut of the door. Plus, playing "You Shook Me All Night Long" never gets old.

☠️ ☠️ $ $ *tried it* ○

321 **BECOME A KARAOKE STAR.** If you've always dreamed of very small-time fame, there may be no better way to achieve your goal than to join the competitive karaoke circuit. Sure, it's cheesy, but the prize may be enough cash to make your public humiliation all worth it.

☠️ ☠️ $ *tried it* ○

322 **WRITE A PORNO.** "I'm not a writer," you're thinking. No worries. By nature, porns have very little dialogue or plot. Throw in a few, "Doctor, what a big tongue depressor you have," a small-town girl looking to make it in the big city, and you're gold. Sell it to a movie studio and you could end up cashing in on the shortest writing gig ever.

☠ $ $ *tried it* ○

323 **DIRECT A PORNO.** Can't imagine yourself doing the nasty on film? Try being the only clothed person on the set of a pornographic movie as the director. There's not much to learn. Your only directions are going to be "faster!" "harder!" and "clean up!"

☠ ☠ $ $ *tried it* ○

324 **STAR IN A PORNO.** Gifted (genetically or surgically) with large breasts or happen to be the owner and operator of a very large penis? Don't deny your gift—become a pornographic actor. While not the type of gig your parents take you out to dinner for landing, if your movie hits it big, you could be the next Jenna Jameson. That's right—no dream is too big.

☠ ☠ ☠ $ $ $ *tried it* ○

325 **ENTER A DANCE CONTEST.** These days, dance contests are everywhere—from televised reality competitions to your neighborhood watering hole. If you can dance worth a damn, try your luck. You could win big bucks or become the laughing stock of the contest. But, hey, you can't control that. As Gloria Estefan waxed poetic, the rhythm is gonna get you.

☠ ☠ $ *tried it* ○

Be a Star

326   **ENTER A RAP BATTLE.** You've seen *8 Mile*. Professional rap battling is an easy way to make some cash, right? Well, maybe if you're Eminem. For the rest of us, it can be a difficult way to make some cash—though not without its merits. An appeal from the general public: only enter one of these battles if you won't embarrass yourself by doing so.

☠ ☠ $ $ *tried it* ○

327   **DROP THAT BEAT!** Timbaland and other producers have made a ton of loot looping and distorting the sounds from drum kits and samples of older songs into beats that rappers and singers then record their lyrics over. Talented in the area of music production? Hit the studio and put together a mix tape of your best beats then shop them around to singers and rappers looking to hit it big.

☠ $ $ $ *tried it* ○

328   **EMCEE AN EVENT.** Monster truck rallies. Beauty pageants. More monster truck rallies. When embarking on a career as an emcee, your possibilities are endless. So what are you waiting for? You can earn a few hundred dollars and learn more than you ever wanted to know about monster trucks in just a few hours.

☠ ☠ $ $ *tried it* ○

Be a Star

329   **DEEJAY A WEDDING.** Folks, if you'll join me on the dance floor, it's now time to join the ranks of the desperate and consider serving as a deejay at a friend's wedding. All you need are some speakers and an iPod loaded with such wedding staples as "Shout!" and "Butterfly Kisses" and you're ready to go. Your friend pays you a few hundred dollars (saving himself thousands) and, if you play your cards right and keep the oldies on the floor, you'll have a job every Saturday for the next year. Congratulations—your life isn't that fun.

☠   *$ $*   *tried it* ◯

330   **DEEJAY A SCHOOL DANCE.** Long for the days when you danced to bad music in the dim light of your high school cafeteria? Take a trip down memory lane while making some cash on the side by deejaying a school dance. But you may be ready to quit the gig before "Stairway to Heaven" ends—kids these days can be a handful.

☠   *$*   *tried it* ◯

331   **DEEJAY A BAR OR BAT MITZVAH.** Get ready to "Hava Nagila" with a room full of thirteen-year-olds. The ages of the guests at bar mitzvahs range from infant to octogenarian, so it can be tricky to satisfy everyone's musical tastes. Be sure to partake in the Manishewitz and you'll be rocking. Advertise your service at local synagogues and event halls and you should be so busy you'll have no reason to *kvetch*.

☠   *$ $*   *tried it* ◯

332 **BE A WEDDING SINGER.** Controversial social commentator Adam Sandler threw the spotlight on the wedding-singing industry in 1998's *The Wedding Singer*. Being a wedding singer has just as much to do with handling drunken family members and pissed-off mothers-in-law as it does hitting the high note in Journey's "Faithfully." If you're a moderately talented singer with time to work on weekends, create a demo disc and drop it off at event venues in your town or city. You'll be singing "YMCA" in no time.

☠ ☠ $ $ $ *tried it* ○

333 **SELL MIX TAPES.** What's old is new again. A well-thought-out and properly executed mix tape was considered a work of art when you were in high school. With the ubiquitous iTunes, there is no need for mix tapes. However, the Urban Outfitters crowd seems to love old, useless crap, and you can make a killing by producing your own mix tapes. Make some sample mixes (with themes like, "love," "break-up," or "party") and shop them around to local gift shops and music stores. They may like your lazy man's mix and decide to carry them in their store.

☠ $ *tried it* ○

334 **BE AN EXTRA.** If a movie is being filmed in your area, consider having your fifteen minutes of fame by being an extra in a movie. There's a lot of hurry up and wait but you may get to rub elbows with a star—and you'll definitely earn yourself some cash.

☠ $ $ *tried it* ○

335 **GO ON A DATING SHOW.** No, you can't be paid to date someone. But if you land a spot on one of those classy programs that houses all the wannabe boyfriends and girlfriends in a house, you can have all your living costs paid for, as well as your travel arrangements. Plus, VH1 seems to give anyone who's ever been on a dating show his or her own series.

☠ ☠ ☠ $ $ *tried it* ○

Be a Star

336 **ENTER A TALENT CONTEST.** Can you sing like Aretha? Staple your genitals to your leg without crying? The general public needs to share in your skill. Enter a talent contest anywhere from your local community center to a nationally televised contest and you could earn big bucks to entertain . . . or just freak people out.

☠ ☠ ☠ $ $ *tried it* ○

337 **DO VOICE-OVER WORK.** Do you have a distinct speaking voice? Consider work as a voice-over actor. It can be hard to get started, but if you get a gig, you can get paid to go to work while you're still in your pajamas. Visit Voices.com to find voice-over jobs in your area.

☠ $ $ $ *tried it* ○

338 **MODEL FOR A LOCAL STORE'S ADS.** Print is print. The experience you receive along with building your portfolio will supplement whatever little money you get for modeling the newest line of outdoors-wear. And who knows—maybe you'll get discovered by some big-shot agent who flips through the fliers for Hometown Sporting Goods when he's back home visiting his mother.

☠ $ *tried it* ○

339 **ACT IN LOCAL THEATER.** Sure it might be off-off-*off*-Broadway, but it's still doing something you love—and are getting paid for (however minimal the scale is for someone putting on *Rent* in Schenectady, New York). Look for audition fliers around the actual theater, or check out its website to see when they're holding tryouts for upcoming productions.

☠ $ *tried it* ○

340 **WALK THE RUNWAY.** You don't have to look like Gisele to get modeling work. Department stores and shopping malls often host fashion shows where they feature real people (albeit attractive real people), as opposed to fashion models, wearing their new designs. If you think you have what it takes, your first step is to get an agent who can take 15 percent of your earnings to get you some real runway time.

☠ ☠ $ $ $ *tried it* ○

341 **BE A BACKUP SINGER.** Feeling a bit more Florence Ballard than Diana Ross? No problem. As a backup singer, you can have the fun of performing without the pressure of carrying the show. Visit your city's craigslist page and search in the "community" section for musicians looking for band members. You'll be "ooohing" before you know it.

☠ ☠ $ *tried it* ○

342 **STAR IN A FILM SCHOOL MOVIE.** Privileged film students love to make bad movies, and sometimes they even have a few bucks to hire some talent (that's you). Drop a picture of yourself as well as a resume touting your acting skills off at local art and film schools and you could experience being in a really low-budget movie. Low budget is kind of the theme here, so be willing to work for cheap.

☠ ☠ $ *tried it* ○

343 **ACT IN A LOCAL COMMERCIAL.** The grainy camera work. The uneven audio. The over-the-top acting. Be that over-actor! Contact local video production companies and tell them you're interested in being in a commercial. When businesses hire them to make a commercial, they'll recommend you, and if you're really lucky, you can be that guy waving in the aerial shot of a car dealership commercial.

☠ $ *tried it* ○

344 **WORK AS A TRIBUTE BAND.** Can you do a good Bono impression? Or do you just really love U2's (or another band's) music? Consider forming a tribute band. With concert tickets to see actual legit bands costing anywhere from $40 to $500, surely you can get a few suckers to pay $10 a head to see you and your friends rock out. Give your band name the same name as the original band's biggest hit or album so that fans of the real thing will be immediately drawn to your act.

☠ ☠ $ $ *tried it* ○

345 **GET YOUR CHILD AN ACTING GIG.** Everyone thinks his kid is cute enough to be on television. But some kids actually are. Is yours one of them? Consider hiring an agent for your adorable little one, and your kid may actually start paying you back for all you've given him.

☠ $ $ $ *tried it* ○

346 **BECOME A CELEBRITY ASSISTANT.** Can you handle being treated like a minion? Do you consider "getting an inside peek at Hollywood life" a job perk? Why not try to get work as a celebrity assistant? Start by contacting management companies (because no one does anything without their manager's permission) and tell them about your career aspirations. Pretty soon you could be fetching double chai lattes for the overpaid and undertalented. Talk about the American dream.

☠ ☠ $ $ $ *tried it* ○

347 **WRITE A SONG.** You don't have to sing or play well to write the next big hit. Rather, pen an original tune with the ultimate goal of having someone else become famous for it. Really, it's not as pathetic as it sounds.

☠ $ $ $ *tried it* ○

Be a Star

348 **FIND THE NEXT BIG STAR.** Whether it's the next big NBA baller or a talentless but wildly successful pop singer, the next big thing is out there. So why not go find it? Attend middle school sports games and talent shows and you may strike gold. The only drawback is the middle school sports games and talent shows thing.

☠ $ $ $ $ *tried it* ○

349 **PITCH A REALITY TV SERIES.** Every new TV season, another half dozen ill-conceived reality shows premiere. Why not think of the next one? Due to the saturation of the market, the trick here is to find a concept that hasn't been used yet. Or just come up with a better name for one that already exists (See: *Big Brother.*) and steal someone else's thunder.

☠ $ $ $ *tried it* ○

350 **TAKE PART IN AMATEUR COMEDY NIGHT.** Okay, so you may get heckled. Or you may wow the crowd and get a regular job doing stand up. Possibly nerve-wracking but always entertaining, this could turn into a career that would keep you in stitches.

☠ ☠ $ $ *tried it* ○

Be a Star

351 **WORK AS A VENTRILOQUIST.** Do you possess the creepy ability to throw your voice? The only way to make it better is to buy a strange-looking doll and involve it in your act. While you may always be known as the person who lives with their hand up a lamb's ass (sorry, Shari Lewis), you'll have the privilege of entertaining the type of people who find that kind of thing funny.

☠ $ $ *tried it* ○

352 **WORK IN A CIVIL WAR REENACTMENT.** You'd think people would rather move past the pain of war but you'd be wrong. Civil War buffs are a devoted group and shell out big bucks to watch actors reenact famous battles. If you think this would interest you (or you just love those funny pants), try getting work in a war reenactment—but leave your musket at work.

☠ ☠　　　$ $　　　*tried it* ○

353 **WORK IN A HAUNTED HOUSE.** If the idea of scaring strangers is appealing to you and you need a temporary job, try auditioning for a role as a haunted house actor. You could end up as a demented innkeeper or a tortured monster. But don't underestimate the possibility of nightmares. Not from the actual haunted house, but the screaming kids you have to deal with nightly.

☠　　　$ $　　　*tried it* ○

354 **WORK IN A RENAISSANCE FAIR.** Do you like fake British accents (Hey, Madonna!) and big ol' turkey legs? Try getting hired as a Renaissance fair worker. The music's not great and the overly enthusiastic coworkers can be a bit wearing, but you can get a pretty good mead buzz while you're making some extra cash.

☠　　　$ $　　　*tried it* ○

355 **PLAY A PART IN A COLONIAL VILLAGE.** Unlike a Renaissance fair (where, oddly enough, people go to party medieval style), most people who go visit colonial villages do so to learn a thing or two. If you're a history buff and like wearing funny clothes, audition to be a character actor. Plimoth Plantation is the crème de la crème of colonial villages, but you're better off working your way up to there.

☠　　　$ $　　　*tried it* ○

356 **BE A CLOWN.** God knows why clowns haven't been out-lawed for violation of anti-creepy laws, but they haven't. So grab your big floppy shoes and earn extra cash on week-ends by playing kids' birthday parties. Figure out how to get started (and earn enough money for a really tiny car) at ClownSchool.net.

☠ $ $ *tried it* ○

357 **BE A MASCOT.** These days, from Little League to the MLB, every team has a mascot. If you want to be the next uniden-tifiable furry animal to get in a fight with drunken fans, consider going to school to become a mascot. Promascot .com will get you started. You'll be leading thousands of fans in the Macarena in no time.

☠ ☠ ☠ $ $ $ *tried it* ○

358 **BE A BIRTHDAY MAGICIAN.** The difference between being a regular magician and one for kids' parties is that you can get away with doing very little that qualifies as impressive. Make a balloon puppy? It's magic! Advertise your services on craigslist (be sure to include a zany and lame tag line) and get ready to mystify (or mildly entertain) a lot of gull-ible little kids.

☠ ☠ $ $ *tried it* ○

359 **FORM AN INTERPRETATIVE DANCE TROUPE.** You may be thinking, "I'm not that great of a dancer." No problem here. Interpretative dance is a snotty code word for, "move around like an idiot." So put on a black leotard, buy a CD of Flemish flute music, grab your ribbon baton, and prepare yourself for difficult-to-understand greatness.

☠ ☠ $ $ *tried it* ○

Be a Star

CHAPTER 7

Write Yourself a Check

Anyone can write a sentence (hopefully). A very select few, however, can make a living by writing. We assume you aren't one of those few. (That's okay—we aren't either.) You can make some extra cash by cranking out some words, though.

360 **WRITE A MYSTERY.** It's not a mystery that suspense and crime novels have gripped the imagination of the American public and you've watched enough *CSI* to have a good idea of how a crime progresses. Make some mad money and write your own. Join the community at the Mystery Writers of America (*www.mysterywriters.org*) to learn more.

☠️   *$ $ $*   *tried it* ○

361 **WRITE YOUR MEMOIR.** How old are you? Who cares? Everyone has a story to tell, and who better to tell yours than you? Pull out your laptop, or typewriter if you're old school, and get going. Check out *www.writemymemoirs .com* to find out how. Just be ready for the repercussions of airing your dirty laundry.

☠️ ☠️ ☠️   *$ $ $*   *tried it* ○

362 **WRITE SOMEONE ELSE'S MEMOIR.** Not sure you have enough to write about yourself. Don't sweat it. Just write someone else's story. Choose a subject/victim, interview everyone they've ever known, and you'll be on your way to the bank in no time.

☠️ ☠️   *$ $ $*   *tried it* ○

363 **WRITE A ROMANCE NOVEL.** Ever wondered what happens when a prim and proper schoolmarm rents a villa in Tuscany and ends up harboring a mysterious fugitive who happens to be the heir to an oil mogul's fortune? Now's your chance to find out. It's the ultimate Choose Your Own Adventure story—with bodice-ripping.

☠️   *$ $ $*   *tried it* ○

Write Yourself a Check

364 **WORK AS AN INVESTIGATIVE JOURNALIST.** Do you have a passion for delving deep into a subject? Did you read a lot of *Encyclopedia Brown* books when you were a kid? Sounds like you'd be perfect for investigative journalism. Be careful though—you don't have the law to protect you, so don't be stupid about who you get your facts from.

☠ ☠ ☠ $ $ *tried it* ○

365 **WRITE A CHILDREN'S BOOK.** How hard can it be? Kids stories barely have words. The truth is, it's harder than it looks. However, if you find a publisher who likes your idea, you could be the Little Engine That Could of children's books. Well, that would make you the second little engine that could.

☠ $ $ $ *tried it* ○

366 **WRITE A YOUNG ADULT NOVEL.** These days, all it takes is a vampire and a little heavy petting to make a bestseller. Don't be mistaken, though—these books are hard to write. After all, who is harder to please than teenagers? But if you have an idea that you think will get you on the bestseller's list, your royalties will ensure you never have to work again.

☠ ☠ $ $ $ *tried it* ○

367 **BECOME A FREELANCE COPYWRITER.** Are you constantly coming up with snappy one-liners? Then this may very well be a great financial move for you! If you read the back of books or sales' print and think you can do better, prove it. If you're not sure how to proceed, check out Freelance Writing (*www.freelancewriting.com*) to find job opportunities.

☠ $ $ *tried it* ○

368 **WRITE WEB COPY.** It's not sexy, but it's practical. Search craigslist or your local online classifieds for part-time copywriting gigs. It helps to be Web savvy and at least partially literate, but you're not trying to be Shakespeare.

☠ **$ $** *tried it* ○

369 **COPYEDIT.** You're the friend who knows where to put the commas and when to use who versus whom. You may as well try your hand at copyediting. You can find copyediting jobs and improve your copyediting skills online at McMurry, Inc. (*http://jobs.copyeditor.com*).

☠ **$ $** *tried it* ○

370 **PROOFREAD.** Grab your colored pencils, kids. It's time to proofread! If you're the type of person who corrects errors in books as you read, you're perfect for the job. It's great to be able to make money off of the mistakes of others. To find proofreading positions, read Sue Gilad's *Get Paid to Proofread: Secrets to Financial Freedom and Success*, or check out online job sites.

☠ **$ $** *tried it* ○

371 **CREATE CROSSWORD PUZZLES.** There's nothing like sitting down to do the Sunday crossword, but why wait until Sunday morning? And why make your friends/family/business colleagues wait either. Put together your own crossword puzzles and make a profit. Check out *www.cross wordpuzzlegames.com* or *www.puzzle-maker.com*.

☠ **$ $** *tried it* ○

372 **GENERATE WORD-SEARCH PUZZLES.** Who doesn't love a word search. They've been used by teacher's for years and keep your mind sharp. You can also keep your mind sharp by capitalizing on America's love of the word search. Feel free to sell your word searches online, or to your friends in books that you can create at Shutterfly.com or Snapfish .com. Check out *www.armoredpenguin.com/wordsearch* to generate your own word searches online.

☠ ☠ $ $ *tried it* ○

373 **MAP SUDOKU PUZZLES.** Sudoku is sweeping the nation, and you may as well jump on the wagon. A great way to make some money is to create a website where you can sell your puzzles to subscribers online. To create your own puzzles, go to *www.sudokucssentials.com, www.sudokuonline .us*, or *www.fiveminutesudoku.com.*

☠ $ $ *tried it* ○

374 **WRITE POETRY FOR GREETING CARDS.** You're a poet and you know it. If you have the skills to write a poem like this, you're perfect for the greeting card industry. If you don't have the skills, you can take an online greeting card writing class at *www.universalclass.com.*

☠ $ $ *tried it* ○

375 **WRITE JOKES FOR GREETING CARDS.** Most greeting card jokes aren't really that funny—which means almost anyone can write them. Having a good sense of humor and being able to write a good one-liner will make you even more successful—and even better paid.

☠ $ $ *tried it* ○

Write Yourself a Check

376 **WRITE PAMPHLETS FOR POLITICIANS.** Welcome to spin city! Some people have a special talent for making every- thing sound good. Can you do that and make some decent money? Yes you can!

☠ $ $ *tried it* ○

377 **SELL YOUR STORY.** It's you your life. Make it pay! Con- tact an agency and see if anyone bites. You have a better chance of selling your story if you have a clear idea of what you want others to learn from listening to you. If all other options fail, you can always come up with something crazy for the *National Enquirer.*

☠ $ $ $ *tried it* ○

378 **WORK AS A LITERARY AGENT.** If you can sell retail, you can sell anything, and you may as well try your hand at selling other people's books. You'll negotiate their salary and take between 10 and 20 percent for yourself. Not a bad deal.

☠ ☠ $ $ $ *tried it* ○

379 **APPLY FOR A GRANT.** Do you have a great moneymaking idea but no way to fund it? Solve that problem by applying for a grant. There are plenty of organizations, including the U.S. government (*www.grants.gov/applicants/apply_ for_grants.jsp*), that want you to have the opportunity to make your dreams come true. You can also check out *www .ed.gov* for more info.

☠ $ $ $ *tried it* ○

380 **WRITE A SCREENPLAY.** Think you've got what it takes to pen the next *Slumdog Millionaire*? Grab a laptop and have at it. The risk is dependent on how far you're willing to go to get someone in Hollywood to read your manuscript. Parachuting onto Brangelina's roof? Well, it was nice knowing you.

☠ ☠   *$ $ $*   *tried it* ○

381 **PREPARE SOMEONE'S SCREENPLAY.** Everyone wants to see their idea come to life. However, sometimes, people have a great story but no writing ability. This is where you step in. For a fee, you listen to your client and write his screenplay. You get a minor credit but major cash.

☠   *$ $ $*   *tried it* ○

382 **ADAPT A SCREENPLAY FROM A BOOK.** Want to make it in Hollywood? Well, here's your chance. Choose your favorite book and get going. If you use a service like Screenwriters Online (*www.screenwriter.com*), you could even win a Golden Globe or an Academy award!

☠   *$ $ $*   *tried it* ○

383 **ADAPT A BOOK FROM A SCREENPLAY.** Oftentimes, studios will release novelizations of popular movies to capitalize on their success. You could be the person who turns next summer's big blockbuster into a book. Your parents will be so proud.

☠   *$ $ $*   *tried it* ○

384 **SELL YOUR CARTOONS.** Pretend you're taking notes in the next meeting you go to at work. In actuality you can be drawing cartoons (or caricatures of your boss) to sell. Make them niche-y to score extra bucks (as in, sell the caricatures of your boss to your coworkers).

☠ $ *tried it* ○

385 **DRAW A COMIC.** If you know how to draw and grew up reading *Spider-Man, Superman,* and *The Fantastic Four,* this may be the job for you. You get to release your creative juices and make a few bucks at the same time. Try to sell your comic to a website or comic book publisher. What's stopping you? Pick up your colored pencils and get drawing!

☠ $ $ *tried it* ○

386 **DRAW MANGA.** This Asian art form is sweeping today's market. Take home your chunk of the change by getting on board and drawing your own. Make a name for yourself by showcasing some of your material online. It's probably a good idea to get an idea of the different types of Japanese animation before you get started, so learn what manga is all about at *www.manga.com*.

☠ $ $ *tried it* ○

387 **WRITE FOR A VIDEO GAME.** Let's face it: you've probably wasted enough of your life playing video games. Now it's time to put all of that (seemingly) worthless knowledge to good use by writing for video game companies. A lot of the time, developers will have the story set, but need someone to write the dialogue.

☠ $ $ $ *tried it* ○

388 **WRITE COVER LETTERS.** Everyone is applying for jobs nowadays, and writing the cover letter is often the hardest part of the process. Avoid having to write your own cover letter by writing them for other people. It'll be pretty easy if you create a template and plug in the info that you're given. Check out cover letter templates at *www.career .vt.edu/JOBSEARC/coversamples.htm.*

☠   *$ $*   *tried it* ○

389 **CRITIQUE RESUMES.** There are tons of resume books on the market today, but why not cut out the middleman and tell your clients what you think. Set up a website and have job seekers send in their resumes and a copy of the job they're looking to apply to. Give them your opinion on their resumes and let them know what they should change. They get the job and you the cash. A win-win situation.

☠ ☠   *$ $*   *tried it* ○

390 **WRITE RESUMES.** Let's face it, resume writing is hard. There are so many ways to create a resume. Should you use bullet points? Is it better to write a job-based resume or a skill-based resume? If you know the answers to these questions, you're well on your way to having another job to put on your own resume. Have clients send you their job descriptions along with their employment dates. Talk to them to find out what their responsibilities were and create a resume tailored specifically for them. Just be careful. You may take the heat if they don't get the job.

☠ ☠ ☠   *$ $ $*   *tried it* ○

Write Yourself a Check

391 **SELL YOUR POETRY.** If you're a gifted poet, consider selling your original poetry to magazines, websites, or even to people looking to give a gift to a loved one. It can be tricky to be successful at selling your poems, but it's much easier than landing a book deal. Visit NetPoets.com to find out how to market your innermost feelings.

☠ ☠ $ *tried it* ○

392 **ENTER WRITING CONTESTS.** Do your friends tell you that you're the best storyteller they've ever listened to? Turn that admiration into profit. Write something, anything and enter it into a competition. Check out *Writer's Digest* (*www.writersdigest.com*) or the Global Short Story Competition (*www.globalshortstories.net*) for details.

☠ $ $ *tried it* ○

393 **CONTRIBUTE TO STORY COLLECTIONS.** You tell stories about your life every day, and you may well make some cash for doing it. With the short attention span of the majority of Americans, story collections are big business. Oftentimes, ads for personal stories can be found in newspapers, journals, or online.

☠ $ $ *tried it* ○

394 **HOST WRITING RETREATS.** Your three roommates just moved out, and you're stuck with the entire lease. Before you start scouring craigslist for subnormal substitutes, think about opening your door to aspiring writers. You'll need to provide them with food and writing materials, but at least that creative writing course you took in college will come in handy.

☠ ☠ $ $ $ *tried it* ○

395   **WRITE AND SELL EROTICA.** Everyone loves a good erotic story—why else would you be reading this book? (Oh, right. Wrong collection.) If you think you're spicy enough to come up with a passionate page turner, investigate which houses publish individual titles or collections for audiences to whom you can write. You'd be surprised at what gets some people off.

☠ ☠ $ $ *tried it* ○

396   **WRITE A SCI-FI CHANNEL MOVIE SCRIPT.** How many times have you thought, who the hell writes these things? Well the answer could be *you*. Think you have an idea for a script on par with *Aztec Rex, Deadly Swarm,* or *Yeti: Curse of the Snow Demon*? Write up an abstract and sample, and send it in to Sci-Fi Pictures, the channel's movie production branch. Careful though, your reputation will get fed to *Frankenfish*.

☠ ☠ ☠ $ $ *tried it* ○

397   **WRITE A STRAIGHT-TO-DVD MOVIE SCRIPT.** These suckers are cash cows. If a studio owns the rights to the title of a successful movie, they'll turn it into an at-home empire (see: *American Pie, Bring It On,* or *Air Bud*). If you have an idea on how to extend a brand—seriously, we think they're on to Stifler's great-grandkid—then put together a proposal and pitch it.

☠ $ $ $ *tried it* ○

CHAPTER 8

Get Crafty

Put those skills Grandma taught you to good use. The magic you work with your fingers is an easy way to supplement your finances—as long as you're good at it. No one wants wool gloves with mis-sized fingers, paintings that look like they were done by kindergarteners, or a haircut fit for your eighth grade gym teacher.

398 **MAKE JEWELRY.** Handcrafted jewelry can be really expensive. While your initial investment may be a bit steep since you'll need a variety of materials, the craft fair crowd goes ga-ga for homemade jewelry. Visit FestivalNet.com to find a craft fair near you and sign up for a booth to sell your homemade baubles (for a big markup).

☠ $ $ *tried it* ○

399 **WEAVE HEMP JEWELRY.** Hemp jewelry isn't just for hippies anymore. You can sell it in any natural or organic store. Find a way to make it seem like couture and you'll convince the rich soccer moms that it's the best thing since Ugg boots.

☠ $ *tried it* ○

400 **MAKE AND SELL JEWELRY BOXES.** As the business of handmade jewelry continues to grow, people are going to need a place to put all those pretty little things. Create jewelry boxes to sell online and at local craft fairs. It's the perfect gift for anyone who has made the Buy Handmade Pledge (*www.buyhandmade.org*).

☠ $ $ *tried it* ○

401 **KNIT SWEATERS.** Turn your hobby into cash. A homemade knit sweater is a great gift. Try selling them around the holidays to get more customers. Offer to personalize them for an extra cost.

☠ $ $ *tried it* ○

402 **KNIT HATS, GLOVES, SOCKS, AND SCARVES.** Create some wooly accessories sets and people will line up to buy them as gifts for the holidays. The tighter your knitting skills, the more you can charge to warm people's ears, hands, and hearts.

☠ $ *tried it* ○

Get Crafty

403 **CROCHET.** A lovely afghan or baby blanket will sell for a nice chunk of change. People like homemade blankets so get crocheting! You can put it up for sale on Etsy.com.

☠ $ $ *tried it* ○

404 **CRAFT BY REQUEST.** How many times have you tried to find a scarf that matches your favorite sweater (or vice versa), but came up empty-handed because you couldn't find the correct color or pattern? Well now you can help others solve this issue by renting out your knitting and crocheting services. Rather than choose the yarn and style *you* want, let others pick—for a higher price.

☠ $ $ *tried it* ○

405 **SELL DECORATIVE PILLOWS.** Some nice throw pillows can really add personality to a room. If you can embroider, a few personalized touches can make a boring pillow something special.

☠ $ *tried it* ○

406 **BEAD BRACELETS.** Remember how fun this was in junior high? You'd give them to all of your friends and it made you the cool kid in your class. Now, take it up a notch and turn your favorite childhood activity into a lucrative business. Attach a cause to it as Lance Armstrong did and you're sitting on a jackpot.

☠ $ *tried it* ○

407 **PERSONALIZE CLOTHES.** Who doesn't want a pair of pants with her name across the butt or a picture of her cat on her socks? Okay, maybe you won't have orders for those, but people like personalized clothing. Find a way to make their item truly special and they'll pay. People want to know they have a one-of-a-kind.

☠ $ $ *tried it* ○

408 **MONOGRAM CLOTHES.** Some people are just full of initial pride. It used to be that this was especially the case for newly married women whose initials had just changed, but these days everyone's all about the initial. And when they're on your clothes you can always remember them!

☠ $ *tried it* ○

409 **BEDAZZLE PHONES.** Don't sell your Bedazzler just yet. Bedazzles aren't just for jean jackets anymore. With everyone's obsession with bling, you're sure to make a killing when you bedazzle people's phones.

☠ $ *tried it* ○

410 **SELL YOUR SCULPTURES.** People pay ridiculous amounts of money on art, and they like to have conversations starters in their home. Create a bizarre sculpture and it's sure to sell. If you don't really know how to sculpt, fake it and call it art nouveau.

☠ ☠ $ $ *tried it* ○

411 **PAY YOUR BILLS WITH YOUR POTTERY.** If you're artistic (beyond that ashtray you made for your nonsmoking mother), consider selling homemade pottery pieces. Check out the latest home design magazines for popular trends, and create pieces that fit into the décor. Sell your wares at craft stores and craft fairs. Visit FestivalNet.com to find the next craft fair near you.

☠ $ *tried it* ○

412 **SCRIMSHAW FOR SALE.** Have a passion for all things nautical and an uncanny skill at carving small details into bone? Combine that love with that talent and make scrimshaw. Originally carved in whalebone, these days you're more likely to get your hand on camel bone or Micarta.

☠ ☠ $ $ *tried it* ○

413 **SELL A PAINTING.** Anything can pass for art. Have you ever seen some of Picasso's later work? Someone is bound to find something meaningful in your work so don't worry if you don't really know what you're doing. Some of the great artists were on drugs most of the time and they made a fortune. Try painting outside—people are always drawn to looking over the shoulder of artists working in public. Have several almost finished canvases and then sell them in quick succession à la *I Love Lucy*.

☠ $ *tried it* ○

414 **PAINT MURALS.** If you see an unsightly wall on a business, offer to paint a mural for them. Target businesses that have a friendly, lighthearted attitude (such as ice-cream shops or children's bookstores) and depending on the size of the mural, you can make a couple hundred dollars a whack.

☠ $ $ *tried it* ○

415 **TAG FOR MONEY.** Graffiti is no longer just for punk kids who like to deface property. Companies will actually pay people to advertise their product or service using graffiti. It's sure to capture people's attention.

☠ ☠ ☠ $ $ *tried it* ○

416 **SELL YOUR PHOTOGRAPHS.** Talk to your local coffee shop about hanging some of your best shots. They get free art on the walls and you get free exposure (no pun intended). Make sure you've got your phone number listed prominently for potential sales.

☠ $ $ *tried it* ○

417 **TAKE HEADSHOTS.** It's one of the easiest forms of photography, and all you need is photography equipment and good lighting. Everyone from high school seniors to corporate professionals needs headshots, and few people are as cheap as Johnny Drama.

☠ $ $ *tried it* ○

418 **SHOOT FAMILY PORTRAITS.** You can spot new parents a mile away. A camera is attached to their head and they're trying to get their one-year-old to sit still and smile for Mommy. When the holidays arrive, the whole family needs to get their picture taken. Set up a small studio in your house or take family portraits in the park.

☠ $ $ *tried it* ○

419 **SELL BOUDOIR PHOTOS.** Scantily clad photos of oneself make the perfect Valentine's Day present. Women need someone they're comfortable enough with to get au natural in front of. Relax them with some chamomile tea and aromatherapy candles, then start shooting.

☠ ☠ ☠ $ $ $ *tried it* ○

420 **SHOOT PET PORTRAITS.** Next to baby pictures, people love to take pictures of their pets. Dress them in up clothes or with props and you'll have customers knocking down your door.

☠ ☠ $ $ *tried it* ○

421 **CREATE PHOTO MOSAICS.** Remember when photo mosaics were really popular? Taking lots of tiny pictures and making one giant picture? If you can find someone else who also remembers this (fondly) get them to pay you to make one!

☠   *$*   ***tried it*** ○

422 **MAKE AND SELL PICTURE FRAMES.** With picture frames, you're not limited in the materials that you use; the only requirement is that there is a hole somewhere to put a picture into. Consider using "found" objects to create frames such as feathers or water bottle caps. Recycled is hot, and cheap.

☠   *$ $*   ***tried it*** ○

423 **DO PERSONALIZED ENGRAVINGS.** Getting something engraved is always a popular gift choice for birthdays, graduations, or anniversaries. It can get expensive depending on what they want it to say, so try to offer deals that professional shops can't offer.

☠ ☠   *$ $*   ***tried it*** ○

424 **CARVE SOME CASH OUT OF STONE.** People collect all sorts of things, one being stone carvings. If you carve out a whole chess set, it could be worth a lot of money.

☠ ☠   *$ $*   ***tried it*** ○

425 **HOCK COUTURE.** If you've ever wanted to become a designer, now's your chance. Advertise yourself as the new Versace and people will pay a fortune. A pair of pants for $700 sounds reasonable, right?

☠ ☠   *$ $ $*   ***tried it*** ○

Get Crafty

426 **MAKE RECYCLABLE FASHION.** Hipsters love wearing used clothes—and they love it even more when it's been somehow combined with other used stuff to make "new" fashion. To find out about local craft fairs coming up where you could sell your goods visit *www.craftster.com.*

☠ $ $ *tried it* ○

427 **CREATE AND SELL REUSABLE SHOPPING BAGS.** Reusable shopping bags are all the rage now. People want to do their part to go green and this is a simple way. They go for $1 a pop at all the major grocery stores. Make some really unique ones or personalize them and charge a dollar extra.

☠ $ *tried it* ○

428 **SELL WIND CHIMES.** A few shells and bells on some clear wire make for a cheap and easy wind chime. Use colored glass beads or hollow metal tubes to create different sounds. Your customers will appreciate your unique ideas.

☠ $ *tried it* ○

429 **SELL HOMEMADE BEAUTY PRODUCTS.** Some vanilla sugar body scrub or herbal face wash sells for big bucks at the mall. You make these products with most of the items in your cupboard and sell them for a big profit.

☠ $ $ *tried it* ○

430 **BLOW AND SELL GLASS.** Blowing glass is a true art form, usually found at a Renaissance faire. If you are a talented glass blower, sell your creations. You can even call up the faire and ask to set up a booth.

☠ ☠ ☠ $ $ *tried it* ○

431   **ETCH GLASSES.** Glasses are super cheap—take a trip to your local Ikea and you can get most sizes for around one dollar. Get yourself a container of etching cream and some fun-shaped stickers and you're all set.

☠   *$ $*   *tried it* ◯

432   **SELL YOUR NATURAL SUDS.** Create your own signature fragrance and sell your soaps to local specialty stores. Soaps make perfect gifts and favors, so you can also market your services to the baby/bridal shower industries. You will be dealing with hot liquids, but you'll be fine as long as you follow the basic safety precautions.

☠ ☠   *$ $*   *tried it* ◯

433   **MAKE AND SELL YOUR OWN SHAMPOO.** If you believe the organic movement, it's only a matter of time before your Pert Plus kills you, so you'll be doing everyone a favor by selling all-natural shampoos. You'll have to do some kitchen chemistry, but nothing on the scale of *Breaking Bad*.

☠   *$ $*   *tried it* ◯

434   **HOCK HOMEMADE PERFUME.** A bottle of Coco Chanel 5 can go for almost $300 at Macy's! In this economy, who can pay for that? Start mixing and matching scents, and make some signature perfume of your own.

☠ ☠   *$ $*   *tried it* ◯

435   **CASH IN ON COLOGNE.** Experiment with some fun essential oils until you've gotten just the right combination. Then tell guys that wearing it will cause girls to rip their pants off, and voila! A successful home-based business is born.

☠   *$ $*   *tried it* ◯

Get Crafty

436 **MAKE AND SELL PATCHOULI OIL.** If you happen to have a patchouli plant growing in your yard, it's time to take it to the bank (okay, maybe it was time forty years ago, but there's no time like the present). You can make this oil by drying out some leaves from the plant and buying a carrier oil (such as jojoba).

☠ $ *tried it* ○

437 **TIE-DYE AND SELL CLOTHES.** Despite the hopes and wishes of much of society, the tie-dye fad didn't die when Jerry Garcia did. Get some cheap T-shirts at your local secondhand store, steal some rubber bands from work, and go to town.

☠ ☠ $ *tried it* ○

438 **MAKE YOUR OWN DYES.** Can't find the color you're looking for at the local arts and crafts store? Make your own! Look around outside—most colored things you find in nature can be made into a pigment. Who knows, maybe other people have also been looking for that perfect "baby rose with hints of carrot yellow" dye.

☠ $ $ *tried it* ○

439 **WEAVE AND SELL TAPESTRIES.** Weaving tapestries can be tedious work. But if you're willing to put in the time, you can charge between $100 and $5,000, depending on the detail work. For extra cash let wannabe tapestrists watch while you work and call it a lesson.

☠ ☠ $ $ $ *tried it* ○

Get Crafty

440 **SET UP STORES' WINDOW DISPLAYS.** Eye-catching window displays draw customers into stores, which is the first step in getting them to the cash register. It's worth it for a store to pay someone a nominal fee to increase foot traffic. Start with local stores; the displays for the chains are usually dictated by the corporate office.

☠ $ $ *tried it* ○

441 **PAINT RETAIL STORES' WINDOWS FOR THE HOLIDAYS.** No $8-an-hour part-time employee wants to wake up early Sunday morning to frost snowflakes on a window. And let's face it, you'd do a better job blindfolded. Start with small stores in your area.

☠ $ $ *tried it* ○

442 **PIECE TOGETHER AND SELL ORNAMENTS.** Some people festoon their trees with ornaments their elementary schoolers made out of pipe cleaners and macaroni. Other people prefer decorations that are, shall we say, identifiable. Take advantage of the latter group by signing up for a booth at a local craft fair and selling your one-of-a-kind creations.

☠ $ *tried it* ○

443 **MAKE WREATHS.** Assemble wreaths for every occasion and sell them through word of mouth or through local craft organizations. Bonus: If you make holiday wreaths from evergreen boughs, your customers will have to come back for fresh ones every year.

☠ $ *tried it* ○

Get Crafty

444 **MANUFACTURE FURNITURE.** You'll be working with power tools; if you have no mechanical aptitude whatsoever, you should skip this one for obvious reasons. If you're handy with an Allen wrench, you might want to offer to assemble premade furniture rather than make an entire bedroom set from scratch.

☠ ☠ ☠ $ $ *tried it* ○

445 **MAKE CRIBS.** It's sort of like a birdcage (see entry 635) or a doghouse (see entry 634), but bigger and a whole lot more complicated. As they say, think "safety first" when designing these cribs. One surefire way *not* to make money is to get sued by angry parents whose baby fell out of your faulty crib.

☠ ☠ $ $ $ *tried it* ○

446 **MAKE MOBILES.** Hang more than one of anything from some string and you've got a mobile. You can get as fancy, minimalist, artsy, or ironic as you want to with mobiles. Finish this sentence: "It would be hilarious to see [blank] hanging above a baby's crib."

☠ $ $ *tried it* ○

447 **MAKE AND SELL STUFFED ANIMALS.** Have extra drapes, pillows, and buttons lying around? Before you think about donating them to Goodwill, consider making stuffed animals out of them. Cut the drapes into shapes, sew together, stuff with pillow stuffing, and sew on buttons as eyes. The best part is it doesn't even have to be cute—Ugly Dolls have opened the door for misfit toys everywhere.

☠ $ $ *tried it* ○

448 **CUT HAIR.** You don't have to go to beauty school to be able to do a quick trim for someone. Haircuts at salons go for $30 to $50 a pop. Who has that kind of money to blow every couple of months? You'll be able to offer a simple trim for a few bucks and you'll get a lot of customers in the process.

☠ ☠   **$**   *tried it* ○

449 **BRAID HAIR.** Everyone gets their hair braided when they go on vacation to a Caribbean island. Those native ladies make a fortune off the tourist schmucks. Braid it before they go and charge them less.

☠   **$**   *tried it* ○

450 **PERM PEOPLE'S HAIR.** Some folks just really want to look like poodles. Who are you to stop them? Getting your hair permed in a salon can cost a couple hundred bucks. Buy a $10 at-home kit, do a trusting friend's hair for free, and tell her to recommend your services when people compliment her on her curls. Charge $75 a whack and you're still offering a huge discount.

☠ ☠   **$ $**   *tried it* ○

451 **STRAIGHTEN OTHER PEOPLE'S HAIR.** Getting your hair chemically relaxed (or straightened) is damaging to tresses and can cost big bucks. Buy a quality hair straightener at a beauty supply store (try SallyBeauty.com) and offer your temporary, less harmful service for $20 a client. Around prom season, offer group specials and you'll be busy.

☠   **$**   *tried it* ○

Get Crafty

452 **PUT IN HAIR EXTENSIONS.** These days, everyone from Brett Michaels to those nitwits on *The Hills* have hair extensions. Getting them put in at a salon can cost big bucks. Quality, real-hair extensions can cost you some start-up, but people will pay you a lot more for them. So turn your shorthaired friend into a longhaired beauty, snap a few pictures, and post fliers around town. You'll be elbow deep in hair in no time (that's supposed to sound like a good thing).

☠ $ $ *tried it* ○

453 **WAX PEOPLE.** This one is tricky. You may end up neatening eyebrows—or having to give a Brazilian bikini wax to a 400-pound woman. It's best to start practicing on friends since you can burn people—and you really don't want to see that 400-pound woman with the burnt hoo-ha mad.

☠ ☠ ☠ $ $ *tried it* ○

454 **GIVE PEDICURES.** People pay up to $50 to have a professional give their feet and toenails a spa treatment. Buy yourself a home foot spa (these go for anywhere between $20 and $200), and offer pedicures to your friends and family. Your initial investments beyond the spa will include nail polishes, foot creams, brushes, and pumice stones. If you're brave, you can advertise your services—but beware of the funky-footed general public.

☠ ☠ $ *tried it* ○

455 **GIVE MANICURES.** As pedicures beautify the toes, manicures beautify the hands. Break out the nail file, emery board, and polish. You might be able to squeeze a few extra "discretionary" dollars out of metrosexuals looking for a nail-buff on the down-low—although these men are a dying breed.

☠ $ *tried it* ○

456 **TATTOO FOR HIRE.** If you're a licensed tattoo artist working at a studio, look into hosting tattoo parties. Groups of friends (or families, if they're related to *Dog the Bounty Hunter*) who want to get inked can do so in the comfort of their own home, and you can make a couple hundred dollars for every person in attendance. Be sure to check out state laws regarding this trend—no one ruins a tattoo party like the fuzz busting in when you're only halfway done with a tat.

☠ ☠ ☠ $ $ $ *tried it* ○

457 **DO HENNA TATTOOS FOR HIRE.** Henna, a natural and temporary dye, is much safer than tattoo ink. Henna parties can be a fun option for kids' birthday parties, bachelorette parties, or even proms. Advertise your services at salons and be sure to perfect a few "signature" tattoos so that you look like you know what you're doing.

☠ $ *tried it* ○

458 **MAKE NATURAL INK.** Get in touch with your old-world self and make some fun-colored ink out of natural resources like berries. Package it with a quill and you'll have Renaissance geeks going crazy.

☠ ☠ $ $ *tried it* ○

459 **WRITE INVITATIONS IN CALLIGRAPHY.** Calligraphy is relatively easy to learn. Take a class and start writing invitations for customers. People pay a lot of money for perfect wedding invitations. Just make sure you know exactly what they want. You don't want to have to redo 200 invitations for a bridezilla.

☠ ☠ $ $ *tried it* ○

Get Crafty

460 **DESIGN INVITATIONS.** Feel like you missed your calling as a graphic artist? Join the club. Make some extra cash on the weekends by doing layout design for invitations (weddings, showers, birthdays, etc). If you don't have a program like InDesign or Quark, see if you can use a computer lab at your local college.

☠   **$ $**   *tried it* ○

461 **LAYOUT RESTAURANTS' MENUS.** You know the scene: you sit down at a restaurant, open the menu, and wait to be taken in by the delicious sounding dishes. But when you crack it open, you're not sure where to start looking—and you can't really read the small type anyway. Offer your services as a layout artist—charge extra for correcting spelling at international restaurants (chiken with kapers anyone?)

☠   **$ $**   *tried it* ○

462 **WORK AS A STORYTELLER.** If you like kids and can spin a yarn or two, consider working as a storyteller. Libraries, schools, and festivals will often hire storytellers to entertain children. You can make up your own or retell classics such as "The Princess and the Pea" and "Rumpelstiltskin."

☠   **$**   *tried it* ○

463 **MAKE ICE SCULPTURES.** Holy chainsaw action! Ice sculptures can be sold to wedding planners (in swan form) and partygoers (in luge form), and can win competitions (in beautiful creation form). For extra fun, play around with colored lights to illuminate your masterpiece.

☠ ☠ ☠   **$ $ $**   *tried it* ○

464 **CREATE BOUQUETS.** If you have an eye for floral design, consider buying loose flowers from wholesale distributors and making your own bouquets. Since the minimum orders from wholesale flower suppliers are usually large, focus your first venture around a big holiday such as Valentine's Day and have your clients order their bouquets ahead of time. The markup in floral shops is huge, so you can offer them a discount while still making money. Just be careful of those thorns.

☠ ☠　　　$ $　　　*tried it* ○

465 **SELL FLOWER SEEDS.** This is an especially good idea if you've grown a particularly rare or special strain of flower. Don't think you have the chops to sell flower seeds? Grow some sunflowers and sell the heads at a local farmer's market for the seeds.

☠ ☠　　　$　　　*tried it* ○

466 **MAKE STAINED GLASS.** Create custom stained glass pieces for people in your community. If you can mimic a famous painting you can bring in the big bucks. Consider doing it mosaic-style; that way you can use scraps from a local glass store and save on your overhead.

☠　　　$ $　　　*tried it* ○

467 **FIND AND SELL SEA GLASS.** If you live near a beach, spend a couple of weekends looking for sea glass. Once you have a respectable amount you can make jewelry or mosaics with the varying colors. Sell them on the beach or online.

☠ ☠　　　$ $　　　*tried it* ○

468 **POLISH STONES.** Get yourself a rock tumbler (or better yet, borrow one from your rock-loving neighbor) and start polishing. You never know what hidden gem might be waiting for you until you've put in the polishing time.

☠　　　$　　　*tried it* ○

469 **MAKE AND SELL NATURAL PAINT.** You can prey on people's sense of fear by spreading rumors (or better yet, truths) about the toxicity of paint. Then sell them your homemade all-natural alternative! It's a win-win situation.

☠ ☠ $ $ *tried it* ○

470 **MARKET YOUR OWN NATURAL CLEANING PRODUCTS.** Studies come out all the time about the dangerous affects of toxic home-cleaning products. Bottle up some vinegar and baking soda and sell it to people who are trying to do some green cleaning.

☠ $ $ *tried it* ○

471 **SELL YOUR KNICKKNACKS.** You know you've got plenty of extra junk lying around the house—tiny precious junk that you can dress up to look like it's worth something. Get creative with it for extra cash (this is called "art").

☠ $ *tried it* ○

472 **WHITTLE KNICK-KNACKS.** People love little wooden figurines. Whether you make Santas for the holidays, or miniature dragons for fantasy lovers, your skills with a knife and soft wood could net you some extra cash. Watch what you're doing though. A little slip and a sliced finger could set you way back in medical expenses.

☠ ☠ $ *tried it* ○

473 **BECOME A FREELANCE ILLUSTRATOR.** Book publishing companies, magazines, newspapers, and websites all need images at various points. Once you have a specific style down, people will come to expect that, so try to remain consistent. And don't think you need to be a world-class illustrator to make money from your drawings. You just need to get yourself seen.

☠ $ $ *tried it* ○

474 **SHOOT WEDDING VIDEOS.** If you have a video camera kicking around the house gathering dust, why not put it to good use by becoming a wedding videographer? You'll need a portfolio to show perspective brides-to-be, so offer to do it for free at friends' weddings first.

☠ $ $ $ *tried it* ○

475 **EDIT WEDDING VIDEOS.** Once you (or someone else) has shot the wedding footage, it needs to be put into a cohesive package. Chances are that the groom would prefer you cut out the part where he gets sick in the bushes outside of the church—or dances a little too close with the maid of honor. Assure him that you can take care of this, but charge extra for it.

☠ $ $ $ *tried it* ○

476 **BIND AND SELL JOURNALS.** Blank books are a popular gift item. What do you get for the person who has it all/you don't know very well? Paper! Bound of course in a gorgeous handmade cover. Trek to your local craft fair or go to *www.etsy.com* for inspiration.

☠ $ *tried it* ○

477 **MAKE AND SELL CURTAINS.** Curtains can be made out of just about any fabric or other material—new or used. Visit your local resale shop and see if you can find some interesting (and cheap) materials to use. You can offer to install the curtains for extra cash.

☠ $ $ *tried it* ○

478 **SELL T-SHIRTS ON CAFEPRESS.COM.** On cafepress.com you can design and sell T-shirts without actually being involved in the creation of the T-shirts. And the best part is that it's completely free! So you really have nothing to lose. Need design ideas? People love to sport pop-culture references on their Ts, especially obscure ones that are generally related to the era when they were born.

☠ $ *tried it* ○

479 **SILK SCREEN T-SHIRTS.** Silk screening gives an artist the ability to make handmade custom T-shirts using their own designs. If you're only making a few of each design you can make individual screens. However, if you're thinking of making large batches, consider hooking up with someone who has a large press.

☠ $ $ *tried it* ○

480 **AIRBRUSH T-SHIRTS.** Airbrushed T-shirts were popular in the '80s and then took a brief hiatus before returning to popularity as urban wear. The ability to mimic graffiti-style is a definite plus, depending on your market audience.

☠ $ *tried it* ○

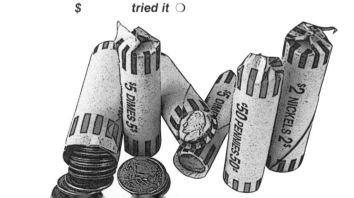

481 **BEAD LAMPSHADES.** When beading lampshades, the sky is the limit. You can make them as small as a candleholder or as big as a chandelier. Make sure that you charge appropriately. Not sure how to get started beading? Check out *www.diynetwork.com* for pointers.

☠ $ *tried it* ○

482 **SELL PERSONALIZED ITEMS.** You can put pictures on just about everything—if you're creative enough. Be it coffee mugs or calendars, mouse-pads or magnets, you can make some money sticking people's pictures all over crap . . . err . . . keepsakes.

☠ $ *tried it* ○

483 **QUILT.** What's more American than a little quilting? Collect material and piece together a patchwork that you can either sell online or at your local craft fair. You could also look to be commissioned to put together a quilt with a particular pattern—and get paid more for it.

☠ $ $ *tried it* ○

484 **CREATE TABLE CLOTHES.** Offer to make people a tablecloth or runner that will match their fine china. Take a picture of their printed porcelain and then head out to the fabric store. Design a table-topper that will make any event in their dining room a show-stopper.

☠ $ $ *tried it* ○

485 **WEAVE WELCOME MATS.** Everyone wants to make a good first impression. Therefore they should be concerned about what their guests wipe their feet on. Have some fun and weave cool designs or funny sayings to really spice up front doors.

☠ $ *tried it* ○

Get Crafty

486 **BOTTLE SCENTED OILS.** Candles are so eighteenth century. Homeowners nowadays are keeping their houses smelling fresh by tapping into the scents of oils. Buy inexpensive, decorative bottles as well as some base oil at your local craft store. Then infuse the oil with all sorts of refreshing smells like vanilla, sage, or cinnamon. Be sure you don't go overboard with the ingredients though—always keep your overhead in mind.

☠ ☠ $ *tried it* ○

487 **FASHION SOME SAND ART.** Bring the joys of the beach to landlocked denizens, or help decorate rental homes up and down the coasts. Find some fun shaped bottles and fill them with sand and other beach discoveries. You could go one above and dye the sand various colors before bottling.

☠ $ *tried it* ○

CHAPTER 9

All about the Hustle

Some people have *it*. Some people don't. If you're one of those people who don't (or don't know what *it* is), you're probably better just skipping over this chapter.

488 **BE A LOAN SHARK.** Bad news: the economy is in the toilet. Good news: you can take advantage of broke people by lending them money at a ridiculously high interest rate. You'll get in trouble if you threaten or harm your clients, but if you can resist the urge to break fingers if they don't pay you back, try this way on for size.

☠ ☠ ☠ ☠ $ $ $ *tried it* ○

489 **SELL RELIGIOUS ARTIFACTS.** Next time you're baking cookies or making a grilled cheese sandwich, put your artistic skills to the test and etch the image of Jesus, the Virgin Mary, or another religious icon into the food. Post a photo of the object on eBay and you never know—you could end up making a fortune off a gullible religious fanatic.

☠ ☠ $ $ $ *tried it* ○

490 **"DISCOVER" A MYTHIC CREATURE.** Those Scottish fools have made a bundle selling pictures and footage of Nessy. And just recently, two guys down South "caught" Bigfoot and had his dead body to prove it.

☠ ☠ ☠ $ $ $ *tried it* ○

491 **SELL YOUR WEDDING GIFTS.** Weddings are pricey. So if you're due to walk down the aisle, register for expensive gifts, only to turn around and return them for cash, or sell them online at a discount price. Sure, you may feel bad selling the cake server your grandma bought you, but you'll get over it.

☠ $ $ $ *tried it* ○

492 **WRITE LETTERS FROM SANTA.** Odds are, you figured out there was no Santa the same way everyone else did: you noticed that Santa's handwriting was very similar to your mom's or dad's. Since typed letters don't suggest childlike Christmas innocence, offer to handwrite official Santa letter responses. Advertise your services near places where kids can sit on Santa's lap—most of those kids can't read, right?

☠ $ *tried it* ○

493 *HO, HO, HO!* **FOR DOUGH.** What would Christmas be without the requisite mall Santa? Less commercialized? Possibly. Less charming? Definitely. Do your part to spread the holiday cheer and pad your pockets by throwing on the fat suit (or just a red suit if you're already padded elsewhere) and work as your mall's St. Nick. Just be careful—you never know what kind of presents little kids will leave on Santy's lap.

☠ ☠ $ $ *tried it* ○

494 **BE SANTA'S SECOND-IN-COMMAND.** While not as glorious of a position as Pai Natal (that's Father Christmas in Portuguese), Claus' elves play an important part in the holiday festivities at the North Pole—and Northside Mall. Who else would take the pictures, line up the brats, and get them to smile?

☠ ☠ $ *tried it* ○

495 **HOP TO IT AS THE EASTER BUNNY.** Almost as popular as Santa and repping a holiday second to Halloween for candy consumption, the Easter Bunny is another lucrative costume to fill. And since you don't have to worry about a holiday shopping rush, it's a lot easier to throw on the fluffy tail and ears than the beard and jingle bells.

☠ $ $ *tried it* ○

496 **WORK A PER DIEM JOB WHEN YOU'RE ON COMPANY TIME.** If you work in a profession where it's possible to get side jobs, use one of your paid sick days and work for someone else. Even if your temporary job only gets you a few bucks, factor in the time you're milking off the company clock and it usually proves to be worth your time.

☠ ☠ $ $ *tried it* ○

497 **SELL YOUR FRIENDS' STUFF.** Next time a friend is moving or cleaning out her garage, offer to help—then keep your eyes peeled for stuff you can sell for profit. She may be planning on tossing out her recliner with the cigarette burn in the armrest, but maybe you can find a sucker on craigslist to buy it for $25. If you feel bad taking advantage of your friend, buy her lunch—just don't tell her why.

☠ ☠ $ *tried it* ○

498 **COORDINATE OTHER PEOPLE'S FAMILY REUNIONS.** Trying to plan a trip or party with your own family members usually results in arguments. So take this annoying task on and create a party-planning company that specifically targets families interested in holding a reunion. Advertise on craigslist and sites like Ancestry.com, and get ready to be diplomatic as you listen to several great-aunts argue for and against the presence of egg salad on the buffet table.

☠ ☠ $ $ *tried it* ○

499 **SELL KNOCKOFF MERCHANDISE.** Paint like Pollack? Sew like a *Project Runway* contestant? Target an overpriced but popular trend; create your own knockoff pieces, then host a party to sell your stuff. If you're any good, you'll be in high demand. If you suck, well, you're going to own a lot of imitation Kate Spade purses.

☠ ☠ ☠ $ $ *tried it* ○

500 **TRADEMARK A BUZZWORD.** Donald Trump actually had the balls to file a trademark request for the phrase "You're fired." So if you notice a term that's annoying enough to become this year's "That's hot," file an application. You could end up cashing in anytime someone uses your brilliant buzzword, though some people may have a few choice words for you.

☠ ☠ $ $ $ *tried it* ○

501 **BUY GOLD AND RESELL IT.** Gold is at the highest price in years, and websites like USGoldBuyers.com are willing to pay top dollar for it. Some people are wary of mailing their gold to a faceless website, so consider buying gold from others and reselling it for profit. Start with people you know ("But Mom, you never wear your wedding ring!") and encourage your first customers to tell their friends. Be sure to check out the *Consumer Reports* assessment of the site you are going to mail the gold to, or the hustler may become the hustled.

☠ ☠ ☠ $ $ $ *tried it* ○

502 **START A DUMPING SERVICE.** Telling your significant other that he or she is not so significant is a sucky task at best. Why not take on this messy chore for others? Sure, you'll end up consoling heartbroken men and women, but they don't have your number to drunk dial you in the middle of the night.

☠ ☠ $ *tried it* ○

503 **LAUNCH A GROVELING EXPERIENCE.** Everybody screws up now and again. But winning back someone's trust can be an annoying and time-consuming process. Particularly heartless people can hire you to do it for them! You'll be delivering a lot of flowers and probably get slapped now and again, but perhaps if one of the unforgiving souls is upset enough, you could get her number and use your newfound cash to take her on a date.

☠ ☠ ☠ $ $ *tried it* ○

504 **START A DATING SERVICE FOR DORKS.** Even dorks need to get laid. Create an online dating site that hooks up like-minded nerds. Give them further incentive to join your site by hosting sessions to help them approach the opposite sex. Advertise online on popular graphic novel fan sites, science fiction chat rooms, and the websites for bad emo bands.

☠ ☠ $ $ *tried it* ○

505 **HIRE OUT AS A RELATIONSHIP ASSISTANT.** Guys need as much help as they can get when it comes to keeping up with the women in their lives. Why not become the George to your friend's Jerry and help stay on top of him meeting his girlfriend's (or wife's) needs? You can keep her schedule straight for him, send flowers and chocolates on special occasions, and remember all those "little things" he always forgets. Just don't get found out—it could be the end of you both.

☠ ☠ $ $ *tried it* ○

506 **TURN TOOLS INTO GENTLEMEN.** Think you have enough style and class to persuade some beer-chugging frat guys to change their ways? Put together a plan and pitch it to them (and their girlfriends/mothers). With the popularity of shows like *Tool Academy* and *From Gs to Gents*, there's definite interest in these male-*Pygmalion* transformations.

☠ ☠ $ $ $ *tried it* ○

507 **BECOME AN EMERGENCY CONTACT FOR HIRE.** Most places of employment require their staff to provide emergency contact information. Yet many people struggle to think of someone responsible enough to saddle with this responsibility—that's where you come in. Market yourself as a reliable, upstanding citizen. Then hit up friends and acquaintances for a fee, in exchange for you becoming their go-to on a crisis. This is easy money . . . until one of your customers has an actual emergency.

☠ ☠   *$ $*   *tried it* ○

508 **PERK UP WALLFLOWERS.** Some people just need a push to be social. Be the one who gives them that encouraging shove. Hire out as an advisor to shy guys and gals who want to take a more active role in life. Be careful though— once you release the beast, you might not be able to contain it.

☠ ☠   *$ $*   *tried it* ○

509 **GET AND SELL CELEBRITY AUTOGRAPHS.** If you live in Hollywood or the New York City area, you may see some stars every once in awhile. Visit popular celebrity haunts and get their autographs, assuring them you're their number one fan. Make sure they don't include your name so that you can post them on eBay and sell them for big bucks. Don't feel guilty—celebrities are some of the most overpaid hacks out there.

☠   *$*   *tried it* ○

510 **LAUNCH A LETTER-OF-RECOMMENDATION WRITING SERVICE.** Everyone out there fudges their resume a bit. But when it comes to letters of recommendation for new employers, there's really no way around it . . . until now. Create a service that allows folks to use you as their recommendation writer. Their potential employers may call you for a quick confirmation, and assuming the unemployed liar has paid you, you can give a glowing review. Ask for a bonus if the person gets the position.

☠ ☠ $ $ *tried it* ○

511 **TELL PEOPLE'S FORTUNE WITH TAROT CARDS.** For some reason, people believe that any idiot with a deck of tarot cards can see the future. Hey, that's not your fault. So get yourself some legit-looking tarot cards and offer readings. Visit LearnTarot.com to get started.

☠ ☠ $ *tried it* ○

512 **BE A PHONE PSYCHIC.** People desperate to know their future will spend up to $4 a minute to have a "real psychic" (i.e., you) tell them their future. By being vague yet encouraging ("I see a favorable year for you"), you can hop on this gravy train.

☠ ☠ ☠ $ *tried it* ○

513 **READ PALMS.** To some, those creases and cracks in your hands actually mean something (not just that you need to moisturize more). They represent lovelines and lifelines and dollar signs—for the person practicing the palmistry. Making money off the practice could be in your future as well, as long as you're convincing enough.

☠ ☠ $ $ *tried it* ○

514 **TEACH COMPUTER SKILLS TO SENIOR CITIZENS.** Even if your computer skills are only so-so, you probably know enough to show a few septuagenarians how to use basic computer applications like Microsoft Office and e-mail programs. Drop your resume off at senior centers and offer group or one-on-one classes. You'll get some cash and, more than likely, a few kisses on the cheek.

☠ $ $ *tried it* ○

515 **BE A PHONE SEX OPERATOR.** For some people, heavy breathing and suggestive conversation is enough to get their rocks off. If you don't mind saying some naughty words for money and you can come up with sexy responses to some out-there questions, be that seductive voice on the other end of the phone. Advertise in the personal section of your city's craigslist page, and be sure to look at your caller ID. You'll have a hard time looking your dad in the eye if you accidentally told him he deserved a spanking.

☠ ☠ ☠ $ $ *tried it* ○

516 **WORK AS A HOLISTIC HEALER.** The organic craze has reached your medicine cabinet, and some people are hesitant to take so much as a Tylenol. Become a natural healer and leave your business card at natural food stores to get a healthy following. Visit NaturalHealers.com for a state-by-state breakdown of holistic schools. Namaste.

☠ ☠ $ $ *tried it* ○

517 **BECOME A GHOST HUNTER.** Dan Aykroyd and Bill Murray actually had to trap ghosts. You just have to locate them, which is pretty easy to do when (NEWSFLASH!) ghosts aren't real. Create an ad touting your skills as a communicator with the spirit world and be prepared to be walked through a few creepy houses. Tell the owner they need to make peace with the ghost, charge 'em $50, and get outta there—just in case ghosts actually do exist.

☠ ☠ $ $ $ *tried it* ○

All about the Hustle

518 **WORK AS A HYPNOTIST.** You're getting desperate . . . very desperate. The next time you have to borrow laundry quarters from your mother, you'll go to *www.hypnosis education.com* to find out how you can become a hypnotist and help desperate souls quit smoking, go on a diet, or find eternal enlightenment.

☠ ☠ $ $ *tried it* ○

519 **SELL MEDITATION TAPES.** Since it's easiest to meditate in quiet, this one is pretty easy. Create a tape or CD of soothing sounds (nature sounds are a good one) and sell them at yoga studios and meditation centers. You may not achieve enlightenment, but you should earn enough money to buy a CD that actually has music on it.

☠ $ *tried it* ○

520 **HOST MEDITATION RETREATS.** Open your house and say "Ommm." If your home is in a peaceful and serene location, offer up your abode to a meditation group looking for a retreat. Be sure to offer healthy and organic meals and make sure they bring their own meditation leader—even you can't fake meditation for forty-eight hours.

☠ ☠ $ $ *tried it* ○

521 **BE A WINGMAN FOR HIRE.** When you're looking to score with an attractive member of the opposite sex, a wingman always helps. Market yourself as the ultimate wingman (including "testimonials" from previous "customers") and post an ad on craigslist or the entertainment section on your city's newspaper's website. Be ready to help out the socially inept, and possibly enlist the help of a hired target so that your efforts don't prove fruitless.

☠ ☠ $ *tried it* ○

All about the Hustle

522   **BECOME A DATING COACH.** You probably know people who have been on a thousand first dates, only to never hear from their love interest again. Hold a coaching session to teach these loveless saps what they're doing wrong. If *you* don't know how to handle yourself on a first date, pick up any old issue of *Cosmo*—there's probably an article that can teach you how. Just don't let your students know that.

☠ ☠   *$ $*   ***tried it*** ○

523   **FENG SHUI OTHER PEOPLE'S HOMES.** People can come up with plenty of reasons to rationalize their crappy lives. One such reason is that their environment doesn't have positive *qi*, or energy flow. Buy yourself a book on feng shui (a good beginner's one is *The Everything Guide to Feng Shui*) and reorganize people's homes so that the flow of energy translates to some cash flow.

☠   *$ $*   ***tried it*** ○

524   **DO ASTROLOGICAL READINGS.** Some people actually believe their fate is determined by their birth date. They're probably wrong, but that's not for you to decide. Hit the Web to find out how to read people's astrological signs and advertise your services at new age stores and coffee shops.

☠   *$ $*   ***tried it*** ○

525   **START YOUR OWN RELIGION.** True, people do seem to get themselves in trouble by doing this. But you're not planning on making any mass sacrifices are you? Think of a few ways you can "save" your followers, and request their "support" so that you can continue to spread the word. Just steer clear of the IRS.

☠ ☠ ☠   *$ $ $*   ***tried it*** ○

526 **WORK AS A LOBBYIST.** You probably have some morals somewhere in you, right? Why not find a special interest group or industry that shares your beliefs and advocate to the government on their behalf. Contract local public relations firms to get your foot in the door. You'll create a climate of change *and* get yourself some change in the process.

☠   *$ $ $*   *tried it* ○

527 **BECOME A CREATIVITY COACH.** Everyone has an idea for a book or a movie. If you're creatively inclined (and don't feel bad taking advantage of wannabe artists), post your profile on CreativityCoachingAssociation.com. As their own website states, CCCA "has not and cannot perform any veri-fication of a coach's background or qualifications." Whad-dya know? You're in.

☠ ☠   *$ $ $*   *tried it* ○

528 **WORK AS A LIFE COACH.** One part personal assistant, one part therapist—100 percent bullshit. Yet thousands of people think they need a life coach. If you're an organized, somewhat sensitive person, help a brother out and coach him to improve his life. Odds are, if someone thinks they need a life coach, they probably do.

☠ ☠   *$ $*   *tried it* ○

529 **CLEANSE HOUSES OF BAD SPIRITS.** Many religions believe that burning sage in a home can ward off bad spirits. And it smells good, so your gullible clientele actually thinks you're doing something besides setting some spices on fire and figuring out ways to spend your easily earned cash.

☠ ☠   *$ $*   *tried it* ○

530 **PERFORM EXORCISMS.** If you see someone whose head is spinning a full 180 degrees, odds are, they need an exorcism. Grab some holy water, a crucifix, and do your best to appear crazy while yelling stuff about the devil. Evil, be gone!

☠ ☠ ☠ ☠ $ $ $ $ *tried it* ○

531 **READ PEOPLE'S AURAS.** Some religions believe that we all emit radiation or light, and that the colors of these lights can reveal insight into our soul. Most believe that it can take years to learn how to read them accurately. You don't have that kind of time, so hop on the web, give yourself an aura overview, and offer to read auras at new age centers or your local community center. Your chakras should be ashamed of themselves.

☠ ☠ $ *tried it* ○

532 **ACT AS A SEX INSTRUCTOR.** Most people want to be better in bed. Why not lead a class to help them do so? While you can't demonstrate the act, you can give tips to people to boost their confidence, in turn allowing them to cut loose more in bed. Be warned: you'll probably have to imagine your students doing the ol' bump and grind, which may or may not be a bad thing.

☠ ☠ ☠ $ $ *tried it* ○

533 **WORK AS A MEDIUM.** Sometimes, the dead are not so, well, dead. And they may have a bone to pick (or a message to send) to the living. If someone is crazy enough to think they're being haunted, well, you're just trying to help by taking their money and telling them that their great-grandmother does forgive them for skipping her funeral for a play-off game.

☠ ☠ $ $ *tried it* ○

534 **PLAY POKER.** While there are tons of different ways to make (and lose) money in a casino, this is where you can really cash in. Warning: only try this if you actually know how to play poker. You could end up losing your wedding ring to a guy named Chiccy.

☠ ☠ ☠ $ $ $ *tried it* ○

535 **PLAY BLACKJACK.** The trick to winning at blackjack (though casinos really don't like it) is counting cards. To figure out if you're fit for a career of card counting, read *Bringing Down the House* by Ben Mezrich. If you're still up for it, start practicing your counting and then head to Vegas. But you know what they say about Vegas: if you get caught counting cards, you'll probably get your ass kicked.

☠ ☠ ☠ $ $ $ *tried it* ○

536 **PLAY ROULETTE.** Roulette is a game of luck. If you're feeling lucky, instead of investing your next tax return, play your money at roulette. You'll either come home a hero . . or leave with zero.

☠ ☠ ☠ $ $ *tried it* ○

537 **PLAY THE SLOTS.** The good thing about slot machines is that you can invest pennies and walk away with millions— but the odds are pretty unlikely. Save your change for a year. If you're still up for it, head to a casino and spend the day playing the slots. If you're not, well, that's a lot of change, so you still have some cash.

☠ ☠ $ $ $ *tried it* ○

538 BET ON HORSES. Horse racing goes back hundreds of years. You can win or lose hundreds (or more) by heading to the track. The big race, the Kentucky Derby, offers the largest payout. But if you don't look good in big floppy hats (and who does?), visit HorseBetting.com to find a comprehensive list of races around the country.

☠ ☠ ☠ $ $ $ $ *tried it* ○

539 BET ON DOGS. They're like horses, only smaller—but the pennies you can win off these four-legged racers are just as pretty. You'll need to get over the whole inhumane treatment thing though if you want to make a wager (many tracks are coming under scrutiny—and being closed—for the way they treat the animals).

☠ ☠ $ $ *tried it* ○

540 BET ON PRO SPORTS. Anyone can bet a buddy $20 on a Monday Night Football game, but if you want to win big, get yourself a bookie. Since these shady characters generally don't advertise their services, your best bet is to head to a sports bar and find out where you can get in on some action.

☠ ☠ ☠ $ $ $ *tried it* ○

541 BE A *MADE* COACH. No one knows how to take advantage of suckers like MTV. Besides drawing you into twelve-hour marathons of *Next*, they created a series called *Made* that features high school students looking to become a new person. Contestants have become hip-hop dancers, motorbike riders, and cheerleaders. If you have a talent that someone would actually envy, then visit the *Made* section of MTV.com. You could make a tomboy into a prom queen in no time.

☠ ☠ ☠ $ $ $ *tried it* ○

542 **START A MARCH MADNESS POOL.** March is the one time of year when the whole country pays attention to college basketball. Consider your office—do most of them know more about *Top Chef* than college ball? Take advantage of their NCAA naiveté and start a pool—skimming an organizer's fee from the pool. Hey, you did have to use a ruler to make that grid so straight.

☠ ☠ $ $ $ *tried it* ○

543 **START A DEATH POOL.** Amy Winehouse. Your grandmother. Those guys from *Jackass.* Odds are, these people are not going to be around much longer. Why not work through your grief and make some money? Start an online death pool and allow users to place bets on the next person to kick the bucket. Keep a percentage of the profit, and get ready for the corpses to start piling up.

☠ ☠ ☠ $ $ *tried it* ○

544 **START AN OSCAR POOL.** It's March Madness for gays. The easy part about this pool is that no one actually sees the crap that gets nominated for awards anymore since most of the movies are boring and, well, foreign. Find the list of this year's nominees at OSCAR.com and start a pool, being sure to keep a cut for you.

☠ ☠ $ $ *tried it* ○

545 **BUY SCRATCH TICKETS.** If you can't beat the old lady holding up the line at 7-11, you may as well join her. Sure, your odds of winning are pretty slim, but all it takes is one jackpot to make all that scratching well worth your time.

☠ ☠ ☠ $ $ $ *tried it* ○

546 **SELL FREE SAMPLES.** Devote an afternoon to cruising the mall for free samples. The jackpot is usually the cosmetic section—those women have fragrances, cosmetics, and hair products they give away in hopes that you'll fall in love with the product. Instead, sell them for cash. eBay is your best bet here, but don't get caught. The samples usually come with the instructions that they're not intended for resale. But you always were a rebel, weren't you?

☠ ☠ $ $ *tried it* ○

547 **SELL COUPONS.** Where's the hustle in hocking cut-outs from paper inserts? Believe us, to make this worth it, you better have the kind of hustle that talks a starving dog out of his bone *and* the kind that gets things done fast. If clipping and posting your findings is taking you forever, don't bother. However, if you can make the rate work with the return, try it out.

☠ $ *tried it* ○

548 **BECOME A MOTIVATIONAL SPEAKER.** Al Franken made his *Saturday Night Live* character, Stuart Smalley, famous for his tagline, "I'm good enough, I'm smart enough, and doggone it, people like me." And there you have the gist of motivational speaking. If a room full of losers can be fooled into thinking they're not, just because you told them so, they deserve to get hustled.

☠ ☠   ·$ $ $ *tried it* ○

549 **SELL WEDDING VOWS.** These days, a lot of people are ditching traditional vows for their own personal take on "til death do us part." That leaves a whole lot of grooms looking for help. If you have writing credentials, submit your resume to wedding planners and event venues, offering your services as a "vow consultant." Charge per word and think of lots of ways to say, "I love you," without ever meeting the intended recipient.

☠ $ *tried it* ○

550 **START A BABY-NAMING BUSINESS.** This isn't just another start-up. You actually have to have the persuasive skills to convince parents-to-be to let you name their babies. Just being "creative" won't cut it—you need to be *dynamic*. (And if you're smooth enough to convince them to do entry 192, you could make a few side dollars from willing companies.)

☠ ☠ $ $ $ *tried it* ○

551 **WORK AS AN EFFICIENCY OPTIMIZER.** Ever heard of an efficiency optimizer as a career choice? Neither did we until we came up with this entry. However, people will pay to make their lives run smoother, cheaper, and better. That's where you come in. Advertise that you'll follow your subject around, take notes on their everyday habits and happenings, and then offer *dynamic* (there's that word again) ways on how they can stop wasting time and money.

☠ ☠ $ $ $ *tried it* ○

552 **WORK AS A "PSYCHOLOGY EXPERT."** It takes a lot of school (i.e., a lot of money) to become a licensed psychologist. But by marketing yourself as a psychology expert, you can be a psychology consultant for people writing articles, for news reports, and even reality television shows (since most real psychologists won't go near those shows). Be careful with this one—it's illegal to misrepresent yourself as a doctor.

☠ ☠ ☠ $ $ $ *tried it* ○

553 **GIVE PAST-LIFE READINGS.** A quarter of all Americans believe in reincarnation. A quarter of all Americans are also obese. Coincidence? Yes. But you can capitalize on the reincarnation folks by offering your services as a "past-life" specialist. Open with, "Who do you think you were in a past life?" Then, during your reading, inform your client that their intuition was right.

☠ ☠ ☠ $ $ *tried it* ○

554 **SELL BOOTLEG CONCERT SHIRTS.** Okay, so technically you're not supposed to sell "official" band memorabilia without a license. So call your T-shirts unofficial and sell them outside concerts. Since the ones sold inside the venue cost up to $75, your $20 knockoff will look like a bargain.

☠ ☠ ☠ $ $ *tried it* ○

555 **CHARGE TO TELL WHAT'S HIP.** It's crazy what some people will subscribe to—and it's crazy not to cash in on their stupidity. If you think you have a good idea as to what's going to be the next big band on the scene, charge people monthly to get CD updates of what they should be listening to. Make sure the subscription costs cover the price of buying the single, blank CDs, and mailing.

☠ ☠ $ $ *tried it* ○

556 **BUY WHOLESALE AND SELL.** Bust out your B.J.'s, Costco, or Sam's Club card and go shopping. You don't need fifty rolls of two-ply toilet paper, so keep what you need and sell the rest.

☠ $ $ *tried it* ○

557 **SELL STUFF FROM ABROAD.** Your recent trip around the world resulted in buying useless souvenirs. Fortunately for you, there are suckers out there who will buy this crap just because it's from another country. Mix in a few foreign words and some local flair and you're good.

☠   *$ $*   *tried it* ○

558 **SEND AMERICAN PRODUCTS TO EX-PATS.** As more and more students travel abroad and graduates take jobs in foreign countries, you can capitalize on their homesickness by starting a service that sends over their favorite things they can't find in their new foreign land. You wouldn't believe what people would pay to receive a package of American peanut butter and Dunkin' Donuts coffee overseas. Just be on top of the whole "customs" thing.

☠ ☠   *$ $*   *tried it* ○

559 **ACT AS A DISASTER PLANNER.** No one wants to think about catastrophic things happening. That's where you come in. Hit up places where you can prey on busy moms' love for their families, but lack of time—like soccer fields, dance rehearsals, and fast food joints. Advertise your preparedness services (from preparing first-aid kits to turning their basement into a bomb shelter).

☠ ☠   *$ $*   *tried it* ○

560 **BE A MAGIC 8-BALL—VIA TEXT.** Get yourself a prepaid phone (you could use your own number if you feel like getting prank calls); put together a catchy ad and post it wherever teenage girls flock; take a monthly fee by way of PayPal; and start responding to questions sent in by text message from those who've paid the price. *Wallá!* You're a cell-phone 8-Ball. Will this actually make you money? *Ask again later.*

☠ ☠ ☠   *$*   *tried it* ○

CHAPTER 10

Mind Your Business

Always wanted to set up shop on your own? What better time to do it than when you're dead broke. There are some ways you can work the money-making magic even if you don't have a dime to your name and you want to go into business.

561 **TURN YOUR CAR INTO AN ADVERTISEMENT.** You can get paid to drive your car around with some signs on it. Check out *www.car-wraps-advertising.com* for more information. They say you can get paid $400 a month just for driving around.

☠   *$ $*   *tried it* ○

562 **TELEMARKET.** You might normally hang up on those annoying calls that almost always seem to happen at dinnertime. Luckily for them, they get paid whether you listen or not. For a few hours a day you could make some phone calls and earn a paycheck.

☠   *$ $*   *tried it* ○

563 **BECOME AN AFFILIATE MARKETER.** Businesses are looking for any advantage over the competition, especially in the economic climate. Link up the business's website to your own and watch the easy bucks pour in. You can also look up clients who would be interested in the company and send them e-mails.

☠   *$*   *tried it* ○

564 **CREATE A COMPANY'S VIRAL MARKETING CAMPAIGN.** Do you remember the mysterious trailers and faux MySpace pages for *Cloverfield*? You can easily do that for any company. Just offer your extensive knowledge of Facebook and MySpace (admit it, you're on those social networks all the time anyway) and you're in.

☠ ☠   *$ $*   *tried it* ○

Mind Your Business

565 **WORK AS A FREELANCE PUBLICIST.** You are a people person and know how to get what you want. Advertise your publicity services directly to the artists who think the publishing, music, or movie company they're working with isn't doing enough to promote their revolutionary book/CD/film.

☠   *$ $*   *tried it* ○

566 **DO OUTSIDE ADVERTISING FOR A COMPANY.** Did you ever hear a jingle on a commercial and think, "I could have written that." Now is your chance. If you're especially creative when it comes to advertising, provide your services for a small company.

☠ ☠   *$ $ $*   *tried it* ○

567 **HIRE OUT AS AN INTERIOR DECORATOR.** If you have a knack for matching wallpaper with end tables, take up a job as a freelance interior decorator. You could even teach clients along the way and charge a bit more for the lessons.

☠ ☠   *$ $ $*   *tried it* ○

568 **CREATE FLIERS FOR SMALL BUSINESSES.** If you have a computer and some decorative paper, you can print fliers for small businesses. These companies usually don't have a lot to spend on advertising so they'll be looking for cheap and easy ways to spread the word.

☠   *$ $*   *tried it* ○

569 **CHARGE FOR DAILY MOTIVATION.** Everyone needs some motivation at some point. How else would Dr. Phil get famous? You can send daily messages in e-mail or text messages that offer motivational quotes. People will pay for positive reinforcement, since it's rarely given at work or home.

☠   *$*   *tried it* ○

Mind Your Business

570 **SELL MAKEUP.** Mary Kay is one of the most respectable makeup direct sellers. As a consultant you'll get to try all of the products. All you have to do is convince some women that a new shade of eye shadow makes them look ten years younger. The convenience of this part-time job is one of the big reasons people do it. They also have the opportunity to make a fat paycheck.

☠ $ $ *tried it* ○

571 **SELL JEWELRY.** Direct sellers like Silpada sell jewelry via parties across the country. You'll take home a percentage of the party total. The more people at the party, the more money you'll make.

☠ $ $ $ *tried it* ○

572 **SELL CANDLES.** Partylite is the premier direct seller of candles and accessories. You can become a consultant, throw parties to show your merch, and make some great money. Go to *www.partylite.com* to learn more.

☠ $ $ *tried it* ○

573 **SELL TUPPERWARE.** Tupperware parties were all the rage in the '70s and '80s. Even today, people love keeping things fresh because it saves them money. Visit *http://order.tupper ware.com/coe/app/home* to learn how to become a consultant and become an expert in the art of food storage.

☠ $ $ *tried it* ○

574 **START AN INDUSTRY NEWSLETTER.** If you have a handle on your business, become the industry's town crier and send out weekly or daily news briefs. Be ready to offer some sort of authority and insight, otherwise people won't sign up. You can try to charge for subscriptions, but your best bet might be to build up your mailing list and then charge for ad space.

☠ $ $ *tried it* ○

575 **GO DOOR-TO-DOOR SELLING KNIVES.** Show off your mad knife skills to persuade potential buyers that they cannot live without your blades. Chop, slice, and dice your way to a profit—but be careful not to lose a finger in the process.

☠ ☠ ☠ $ $ $ *tried it* ○

576 **SELL T-SHIRTS IN CONCERT PARKING LOTS.** People still buy T-shirts at concerts even though they go for $40–$50 a pop. You can offer them for half the price and get more customers. Buy a silkscreen machine and make some of your own. Try not to get caught by the band's crew. You'll be taking away from their sales.

☠ ☠ ☠ $ $ *tried it* ○

577 **BECOME A CLUB PROMOTER.** Club owners are always looking for ways to get people in the door. That even includes paying psudo-celebs like Brody Jenner and Lauren Conrad to show up for five minutes to just stand there. If you're a club regular and know the right people, you could be a promoter.

☠ ☠ $ $ $ *tried it* ○

578 **BECOME A PARTY PLANNER.** A good party is not always an easy thing to accomplish. If you're organized and know how to have a good time, plan a party for someone or a company.

☠ ☠ ☠ $ $ $ *tried it* ○

Mind Your Business

579 **BECOME AN EVENT ORGANIZER.** You already have experience putting together the Alpha Delta Pi Rush Week mixer—why not parlay those skills into a full-time gig? You can put on all sorts of events for people, like weddings, birthdays, and concerts. Get your name out there on social network sites and in the craigslist forums.

☠ ☠ $ $ $ *tried it* ○

580 **THROW BACHELOR/BACHELORETTE PARTIES.** People want their bachelor/bachelorette parties to be memorable even if they probably won't remember them in the morning. Think of activities more unique than strippers and shots. If you throw an awesome party, word will travel fast.

☠ ☠ $ $ $ *tried it* ○

581 **PLAN WEDDINGS.** Wedding planners can make some serious dough. Beware that you might have to deal with some pushy brides along the way. Just do what they want and it will make your life a lot easier.

☠ ☠ ☠ $ $ $ *tried it* ○

582 **BE A SHOT GIRL.** You might feel a little sleazy when drunk guys stick dollar bills in your pants just for a shot, but you'll make a fortune in tips. Just tuck away your morals for the night and flirt like hell.

☠ ☠ ☠ $ $ *tried it* ○

583 **DO IN-STORE LIQUOR PROMOTIONS.** Did you know you can actually get paid to promote a specific company's booze? Search online or ask your local liquor store for contact info of a company that needs promoters. You can host tastings for a few hours and make a good paycheck.

☠ $ $ *tried it* ○

584 **WORK OUT A COMMISSION FOR BRINGING BUSINESS TO LOCAL STORES.** You might have a fantastic idea in the back of your mind. Share it with a store in your area and ask for a small commission if their patronage increases.

☠ ☠ $ $ *tried it* ○

585 **WORK AS A MATCHMAKER.** Everyone wants to find his or her perfect match, but some people don't know how to start or don't have the time. Make a list of people you know whom your clients might like. Or take them out to a bar or club and start up conversations.

☠ ☠ $ $ $ *tried it* ○

586 **BUY A RENTAL PROPERTY.** The real estate market is in a crisis. Since no one can afford to buy, people have to rent. If you have enough to pick up a cheap piece of property, rent it out. This goes for commercial property as well. Now is the time, so take advantage.

☠ ☠ ☠ $ $ $ $ *tried it* ○

587 **HIRE OUT YOUR JOB-SEARCH SKILLS.** With people being laid off left and right, they need help finding new jobs. If you're at the computer most of the day anyways, you can make a few quick searches for customers.

☠ $$ *tried it* ○

588 **BUY AND SELL ART.** You know the difference between a master who painted a beautiful abstraction and an "artist" who threw paint with no direction. Congratulations—you meet the qualifications of being an art dealer (as long as you also have a handle on an inflated sense of self-worth). Go to open galleries and search online for undiscovered talent that art aficionados will love.

☠ ☠ $ $ *tried it* ○

589 **DAY TRADE.** Buy low; sell high; trade regularly. It's never been easier to act as your very own stock broker. You can use the Internet to keep track of your stocks as well as buy and sell when the timing's right. (You do however need a handle on what you're doing—otherwise you'll be losing money rather than making it.) A little tip for you: Campbell's soup stock didn't drop when the stock market plummeted.

☠ ☠ ☠ $ $ $ *tried it* ○

590 **PARTICIPATE IN THE CURRENCY EXCHANGE.** With this roller coaster ride of a global economy providing ups and downs and enough corkscrews to make you barf, you should consider cleaning up by trading currencies. You need to keep on top of which country's coin is plunging or rising.

☠ ☠ ☠ $ $ *tried it* ○

591 **BUY PENNY STOCKS.** You wasted your money on a huge level by trusting the shady business practices of Wall Street, so now what do you do? You invest in low-investment penny stocks. Just watch out for fraud because, after all, you are dealing with stockbrokers.

☠ ☠ ☠ $ $ *tried it* ○

592 **WORK AS A PERSONAL STYLIST.** If you obsessively watch *What Not to Wear* and constantly advise your friends on their hair, makeup, and wardrobe decisions (and you're right), this is the job for you. Look for job listings online or just charge your friends for making them look smoking hot.

☠ $ $ *tried it* ○

593 **BE A PERSONAL SHOPPER.** You have spent hours of time reading about the latest fashion trends and yet have no money to actually buy those clothes. Why not give advice to clueless shoppers? You'll help train-wrecks with their style and earn enough for that new Versace what-have-you.

☠ $ $ *tried it* ○

594 **BE A WARDROBE CONSULTANT.** Start with your trusted clients from your current retail job, post a listing on craigslist, and build your client base. Help the fashion unconscious realize what styles flatter their body types. But be warned: Those who can't tell a pashmina from a parka need not apply.

☠ ☠ $ $ *tried it* ○

595 **BE A FINANCIAL CONSULTANT.** Can you explain the difference between a 401(k) and a Roth IRA? Congratulations, you're well on your way to becoming the savior of the financially illiterate! Get licensed and set up shop. But just remember that one bad move can cost a client a fortune—and you your career.

☠ ☠ ☠ $ $ $ *tried it* ○

596 **BE A BLOG CONSULTANT.** Everyone wants to write a blog to keep the world updated on the adventures of their pet hamster, but there are a surprising number of people who aren't Web-savvy enough to make it happen. You can charge a fee to critique design and content.

☠   *$ $*   *tried it* ○

597 **CREATE LOGOS FOR LOCAL BUSINESSES.** Your doodles are better than the logos of most companies. Put your InDesign and PhotoShop skills to use. Contact local companies and pitch them potential replacement logos. If they're at all business-savvy—and you actually do have talent—they'll automatically sign you up.

☠   *$ $*   *tried it* ○

598 **WRITE BUSINESS PLANS.** Have a handle on how to pitch a business to a potential investor? Help scores of would-be small business owners land loans by working with them to develop, fine-tune, and pitch their business plans—for a profit on your end, of course.

☠ ☠   *$ $*   *tried it* ○

599 **BUY AND SELL SPORTS MEMORABILIA.** Some people never know what kind of treasure they're sitting on—or in this case sleeping on with that shoebox full of baseball cards under their bed. Take them off of their hands (for a price, of course), and then resell whatever you purchase (for a higher price, of course).

☠   *$ $*   *tried it* ○

600 **START A GIFT-BUYING BUSINESS.** How's a mom supposed to buy a gift for her teenage son that he's not going to scoff at? Or a husband supposed to find his wife something that she's not just going to return behind his back? They hire *you*—that's how! If you always seem to get gifts for people that really please, market yourself as a professional gift buyer and make some money.

☠   *$ $*   *tried it* ○

601 **RUN A GIFT-BASKET BUSINESS.** Skilled in the art of arrangements? Go ahead and start a service that puts together gift baskets for various occasions. Whether it's baby showers or birthdays, if you have a knack for piecing together one-of-a-kind gifts, put it to use. Just make sure you factor in the component costs as well as any shipping overheads before you set the basket price.

☠   *$ $*   *tried it* ○

602 **START A CARE-PACKAGE SERVICE.** With millions of students living away from home during college and thousands of soldiers deployed overseas, there is a definite need for quality care packages. Pick a theme for the care packages, put them in a hand-decorated box, and sell them to people who care enough to send your very best.

☠   *$ $*   *tried it* ○

603 **DO TAX RETURNS.** Rather than let tax season stress you out, allow it to earn you a few bucks. If you're good with numbers and understand all of those confusing forms, offer to do others' taxes for a fee. You can advertise on craigslist or put fliers up at work—just make sure your "expertise" doesn't cause an audit.

☠ ☠ ☠   *$ $ $*   *tried it* ○

604 **CANVAS NEIGHBORHOODS FOR POLITICIANS.** Can you make a difference in the world? Well, maybe you should ask Barack Obama—a successful neighborhood canvas campaign helped him become *President* Barack Obama. Also, politicians have a wealth of donations, which translates into more money to offer you to go door to door for them.

☠ $ $ *tried it* ○

605 **HIRE OUT AS A MASSAGE THERAPIST.** You've been told you have magic hands. Well then, it's only polite to spread the magic. Place ads online—but be careful people don't think they'll be getting a happy ending. Also, you should get licensed, even if you do have the Casanova's hands.

☠ ☠ $ $ *tried it* ○

606 **CHARGE FOR REIKI.** Now's the perfect time to capitalize on people in need of assisted relaxation and revitalization. Bring them over to your house and let the healing begin. Make sure your customers pay up front, though, just in case it doesn't work.

☠ ☠ $ $ *tried it* ○

607 **HIRE OUT AS A RAW FOODIST.** You were eating uncooked food *way* before it was cool and have devoted your life to it. Share your love for this tepid diet with newly enlightened raw foodies by charging for in-home demonstrations of how to tear it up in the kitchen—without turning on the oven.

☠ $ $ *tried it* ○

608 **SPRAY ON TAN FOR OTHERS.** Who has time nowadays to go to the beach? And with all these safety concerns about damaging UVA and UVB light—who wants to risk their skin with too much exposure to the sun? Capitalize on people's choice to opt out of the "fake-and-bake" cancer-beds by applying tanning cream and sprays for them. If they ask why their skin turned yellow instead of bronze, tell them it's the new *Simpsons*-themed spray.

☠ ☠ $ *tried it* ○

609 **INVENT THE NEW MIRACLE DRUG.** You've seen those infomercials and said to yourself, "I could bullshit people much better than these fools." Well, you're right! Experiment in your kitchen and come up with the new miracle drug that will cure such things as insomnia and/or diarrhea (as well as cause side effects like insomnia and/or diarrhea).

☠ ☠ ☠ $ $ *tried it* ○

610 **BABY-PROOF HOUSES.** First-time moms-to-be are a paranoid bunch, and are willing to open up their wallets to welcome their bundles of joy as best as possible. (Repeat mothers, not so much.) Take advantage of their worrisome nature and cash in when they hire you to hook them up with a safe haven. But beware—your ass is on the line if their little miracle manages to pry the safety plugs out of the socket and stick two pennies in there.

☠ ☠ ☠ $ $ *tried it* ○

611 **OVERSEE A STUDENT'S COLLEGE-APPLICATION PROCESS.** Teenagers aren't the most reliable group you'll ever encounter. Yet they're often left in charge of their college application process. With parents too busy to help out and guidance counselors saddled with several hundred students, you can help out these college-bound hopefuls by overseeing their application process. Depending on how much parents are willing to pay you, you could travel to different schools, help out with the essay writing, and keep track of the various deadlines. Think of yourself as a guidance counselor 2.0.

☠ $ $ *tried it* ○

612 **GO DORM SHOPPING FOR INCOMING FRESHMEN.** If you've ever sent a kid off to college, you know how nerve-wracking this experience can be. Therefore you wouldn't be surprised that people actually hire others to take care of it for them. (These are the same people who don't need to bother with the whole "student loan" thing.) Organize yourself in a professional manner and begin soliciting clients. We suggest starting in and around college campuses at the time they have accepted-student days, or orientations.

☠ $ $ *tried it* ○

613 **RENT BOUNCE HOUSES.** Bounce houses, moonwalks, whatever you want to call them, there's nothing more fun than jumping around in one until you puke. Okay, maybe that was only fun when you were seven. The fun part now is making money off of those vomit houses. Check out *www.bouncersdirect.com* to find out how to buy your own.

☠ ☠ $ $ *tried it* ○

614 **START A CLUB AND CHARGE FOR MEMBERSHIP.** It can be anything from Scottish heritage to astronomy to beer— whatever you're passionate about. Start a club and have members pitch in for snacks and materials. If you're a big enough expert on a particular subject, you'll be able to pull off charging for your very presence.

☠ ☠ $ *tried it* ○

615 **ORGANIZE AND CHARGE FOR SPECIAL INTEREST TRIPS.** There are hundreds of walking/biking/rollerblading tours of New York City. Create your own specialized tour itineraries and advertise one-on-one tours of the city. Don't live in a city? That's okay. Organize hiking trips instead.

☠ $ $ *tried it* ○

616 **PLAN OTHER PEOPLE'S TRIPS.** Everyone loves going on vacation. Not too many people like planning for it. If you're one of the few who gets their jollies by beating the budget travel sites and finding deals on your own, offer your service to those you know who just want to get to St. Thomas, and not spend their lunch break trying to find the cheapest fare and lodging. But be warned: ruin a person's vacation and you're likely to have ruined a friendship.

☠ ☠ $ $ *tried it* ○

617 **ASSESS UTILITY USE.** Some people spend a fortune on electricity and heat when they shouldn't have to. If you know how to cut corners to cut consumption, share those skills with the world. Put together an ad for your services and post online. Don't worry about your success rate—the people who respond are used to wasting money.

☠ $ $ *tried it* ○

618 **BECOME A CAREER CONSULTANT.** The best part about consulting is that it can be done over the phone or over e-mail. Therefore you can carry on a consulting gig while working your real job. If you're skilled at resume building, cover-letter writing, and searching the job sites, help others decide what they *really* want to do with their lives and get them on the right track.

☠ $ $ $ *tried it* ○

619 **BE A "GREEN" CONSULTANT.** Capitalize on the latest trend ("going green") as well as the second-latest one ("consulting"). Whether you offer your services to offices looking to be a little more eco-friendly, or households run by earth-loving moms, you can charge a nice dime showing others how to reduce their carbon footprint. Just don't get found out for driving to and from appointments in a gas-guzzling SUV, doing all your work in hardcopy on nonrecycled paper, and drinking your ten morning coffees out of individual Styrofoam cups.

☠ ☠ ☠ $ $ $ *tried it* ○

620 **WORK AS AN IMAGE CONSULTANT.** Sometimes people wake up and decide they want to be someone else. Granted, most of these people are teenagers, but we digress. Cash in on those looking to make a significant life change by evaluating the image they are putting out there and offering suggestions on how to tweak it.

☠ ☠ $ $ $ *tried it* ○

621   **RUN A CONCIERGE SERVICE.** You don't have to work in a hotel to tell people what's hip in your city. Establish yourself as the go-to-guy (or -girl) when it comes to what to do. Charge either a per-use fee, or establish some sort of subscription that allows people to call you up whenever they want to eat at a great restaurant, or party at a happening bar. You better actually know what's going on—or else your service will be short-lived.

☠ ☠ $ $ *tried it* ○

622   **OPEN A BAR.** Every group of friends in their twenties has talked about opening a bar together at one point or another. Don't let those twentysomething dreams go to waste. If you really think you have what it takes to open your own watering hole, go for it.

☠ ☠ ☠ $ $ $ $ *tried it* ○

623   **START YOUR OWN RESTAURANT.** There's a lot that goes in to opening a restaurant. The first of which is money. See if you can organize a group of investors to go in on your concept and provide some capital to launch. Make sure you have a prime location and great fare. Maybe look into hiring someone who took up menu planning from entry 947.

☠ ☠ ☠ ☠ $ $ $ $ *tried it* ○

624   **OPEN A FRANCHISE.** While not as risky as a one-off restaurant since there's already a fan-base, opening up a franchise is still a risky endeavor—and one that requires some serious up-front cash. However, if you have the financial backing and think you have a spot that works, give it a try.

☠ ☠ ☠ $ $ $ $ *tried it* ○

CHAPTER 11

The Call of the Wild

Whether it's working with animals or out in the wilderness, harness your inner mountain man and answer nature's call to make some cash. If you're afraid of heights or hairy beasts, these might not be the best options for you.

625 **DOG SIT.** Spend a weekend with man's best friend. There's nothing wrong with enjoying someone else's home while watching their pets. You get paid, get some exercise, and get a built-in weekend companion to boot. Register your dog sitting skills online at *http://petsitusa.com*.

☠ $ $ *tried it* ○

626 **WALK DOGS.** Take advantage of other people's full-time jobs and spend your days roaming the streets with your own dog pack. Seriously though, dog walking is big business. Everyone wants to make sure their precious pups are walked and watered while they're stuck at the office . . . and you're just the person for the job.

☠ $ *tried it* ○

627 **SET UP A DOG WASH.** Get down and dirty cleaning up those disheveled dogs. Due to the fact that wet dogs are smelly and leave that smell everywhere when they inevitably escape from the bathroom, people dislike washing their dogs at home. To solve this problem, dog washes began in California and are now popping up all around the country—which is good news for you. Check out *www.thatdirty dog.com* to get advice from dog washing experts.

☠ $ $ *tried it* ○

628 **BECOME A DOGGY STYLIST.** You cut your sister's hair when you were little. Take that experience and use it to your advantage. Each type of dog hair (poodle, collie, terrier, etc.) has a grooming style specific to its breed. To maximize the amount of money you can make and to avoid pissing off your clients, get your different cuts down by referencing *www.seefido.com*.

☠ ☠ $ $ *tried it* ○

629 **TEACH DOGS TRICKS.** Who says you can't teach an old dog new tricks? You can—and you can make big bucks doing so. These days everyone believes that bad dogs are good dogs just waiting to be trained correctly. Make sure to print out a certificate of completion for the proud pooch and owner.

☠   *$ $*   *tried it* ○

630 **BECOME A FOUR-STAR GENERAL AT A CANINE BOOT CAMP.** You're tough right? Who better to teach a pack of pups good manners. Prove to these pooches that you're the alpha and rake in the dough. The number of crude canines you take on will determine your payout—as well as how many times you're bitten.

☠ ☠ ☠   *$ $ $*   *tried it* ○

631 **RAISE AND SELL PUREBRED PUPPIES.** No one can resist a puppy—and you can take this weakness to the bank. There are some start-up costs to this venture, but you'll more than make up for this once your puppies are ready to find new homes. Protect yourself and register with the American Kennel Club (*www.akc.org*) to avoid the "backyard breeder" label.

☠ ☠ ☠   *$ $ $*   *tried it* ○

632 **BREED AND SELL DESIGNER DOGS.** Labradoodle? Puggle? Jack-a bee? Sounds funny, but you won't be laughing when you head to the bank to deposit your paycheck. Designer dogs are the result of the breeding of two different types of purebred pups. Made popular by celebrities like Paris Hilton, they are the hot dog of the twenty-first century. Be sure to register your litter with the American Kennel Club (*www.akc.org*) to validate your investment.

☠ ☠ ☠   *$ $ $*   *tried it* ○

633 **GIVE PET PEDICURES.** Remember back when dogs actually walked the streets wearing nothing but fur? Or when cats didn't wear blinged-out collars? These days, it seems like everyone with a pet wants to spend their money on something unnecessary. Take advantage of these people by giving their pets pedicures. You have to be careful when cutting their nails, so consider buying a PediPaw (*www.pedipaws.com*) so that you keep these spoiled pets happy and safe.

☠ ☠ $ *tried it* ○

634 **BUILD DOGHOUSES.** If you can nail two boards together, you can build a doghouse. Paint them fancy colors and sell them at craft fairs or out of your front yard. Take custom orders and paint dog houses to match owner's houses.

☠ $ $ *tried it* ○

635 **BUILD BIRDCAGES.** Get crafty with wire and build couture birdcages. Or, take it one step further and make bird mansions. People pay top dollar to keep their pets in the lap of luxury. Put yourself in the lap of luxury by inflating your prices in wealthier areas.

☠ $ $ *tried it* ○

636 **MAKE AND SELL BIRDHOUSES.** If you can make a doghouse (see entry 634), you can make a birdhouse. Take a page from that book and make custom houses that match the house you're selling it to. People love things in mini!

☠ $ $ *tried it* ○

637 **FEED THE BIRDS!** When it comes down to it, birdseed is just seeds and pellets. Buy a bag and sift through to check what's in it, then order the individual seeds in bulk and voila! Homemade birdseed, complete with your logo and phone number in case they need a birdhouse to put that birdseed in (see entry 636).

☠   **$**   *tried it* ○

638 **MANUFACTURE PET CLOTHES.** If it looks cute on kids, it will look even cuter on a dog. Get creative with fashions ranging from pajamas to hoodies to rain slickers. The more likely the owner has a matching piece in their wardrobe, the more likely it will become a must-have for pups from coast to coast.

☠   **$ $**   *tried it* ○

639 **DESIGN AND SELL DOG SHOES.** Somewhere right now there is someone Googling "doggie patent leather Mary Janes." Don't believe me? Check out *www.swankpets.com*. Did I mention they sell for $59? (Set of four, of course.) Come up with a shoe-style typically only worn by humans, translate it to Fido-fashion, and watch the money roll in (while listening to the exclamations of "Oooooh! Shoes for dogs!!!! How adorable!").

☠   **$ $**   *tried it* ○

640 **RUN A CORN MAZE.** Corn mazes are fun for the whole family—until you've been in it for four hours, it's raining, and a way out is nowhere in sight. Get yourself a really high chair and you can be witness to the family meltdowns that will undoubtedly occur. For extra bucks, grow some pumpkins (see entry 779).

☠   **$ $**   *tried it* ○

The Call of the Wild

641 **HUNT FOR FOSSILS.** Who didn't want to throw on some cargo shorts and canvas for prehistoric bones when *Jurassic Park* came out? Live out your dreams and take in some dollars by leading wannabe-paleontologists out on expeditions to uncover the newest species of dinosaur. Of course, if anyone does find a set of prehistoric bones—you get a cut.

☠ ☠ $ $ *tried it* ○

642 **GIVE SWAMP TOURS.** Start up your fan-boat and get ready to give some tours of the ol' bayou. As travelers yearn for "real" cultural experiences, they're willing to go to great (and disgusting) lengths to experience it. Speed them through the tall grass—just don't lose any to the gators.

☠ ☠ ☠ $ $ *tried it* ○

643 **SELL PET TOYS.** People take pet ownership as seriously as parenting. That's why homemade pet toys are a very lucrative business. Owners want to make sure that Rover's playing with something safe—and not something that's covered in lead paint. Make your toys for a specific animal, and play up the features you know they like.

☠ $ *tried it* ○

644 **RAISE EXOTIC PETS.** Love unique animals? Turn this passion into profit. The good thing about raising exotic animals is that the money you can bring in is exponentially greater than what you can earn breeding ordinary animals. However, the risk is that you can spend a lot money raising animals that need extra care and attention.

☠ ☠ ☠ $ $ $ *tried it* ○

645 **TAKE PEOPLE ON A SAFARI.** Lots of people want to get a glimpse of the great outdoors. They just want to do it from the safety of a bus or jeep. Make sure to check local laws regarding how close you can get to wildlife on certain types of land like state parks.

☠ ☠ ☠ $ $ $ *tried it* ○

646 **SELL ANIMAL URINE.** You wouldn't believe how much a little animal pee can go for. Homeowners use it to scare away pests and hunters use it to lure in prey. Your level of daring to collect different samples from bigger beasts will increase your take.

☠ ☠ ☠ $ $ *tried it* ○

647 **GO SMALL-GAME HUNTING.** Whether it's ducks, rabbits, pheasants, or any other type of tiny, meaty creature, you can make some money by shooting and selling small game.

☠ ☠ $ $ *tried it* ○

648 **GO BIG-GAME HUNTING.** Big-game hunting can be much more challenging: think sitting frozen in a tree for hours on end before you even catch a glimpse of the bear/moose/ other large animal. Hunters say that this is very peaceful though, so get in touch with your Zen side—until it's time to shoot.

☠ ☠ ☠ $ $ $ *tried it* ○

649 **CAT SIT.** The only thing easier than dog sitting is watching someone else's cats for a few days. Dogs want company and companionship. Cats want you to feed them and leave them alone. They may make you feel unwelcome, but at least you're getting paid.

☠ $ *tried it* ○

The Call of the Wild

650 **BECOME A CAT FANCIER.** Love cats? You're not alone, which is why breeding, and selling fancy felines is big money. Cats can have one to eight kittens per litter and two to three litters per year. It's possible for one single cat to have close to 100 kittens in her lifetime. If that's not a moneymaker, I don't know what is. Check out the Cat Fancier's Association, Inc. (*www.cfainc.org*) for more info.

☠   **$ $ $**   *tried it* ○

651 **GROW AND SELL CATNIP.** It's like marijuana for your cat—but legal to grow and sell! Kitties go crazy for the grass. Pair it with a cute package design and you'll have crazy cats—and their owners—begging you for more.

☠   **$ $**   *tried it* ○

652 **MAKE AND SELL NATURAL PET FOOD.** The natural pet food industry has been booming ever since numerous pooches bit the dust by eating tainted doggy treats. Cash in by selling your own brand of natural, homemade pet food.

☠   **$ $**   *tried it* ○

653 **RUN A PET SPA.** These days dog owners will pay more for the pampering of their pooches than for themselves. Capitalize on this trend by running a pet spa. You can offer Doga classes (yoga for dogs) and services like scalp massages and pedicures.

☠   **$ $ $**   *tried it* ○

654 **BE A PET PSYCHIC.** People need pet psychics for lots of reasons: to help discover where a lost pet might be hiding out, to make sure that Snowball isn't suffering in purgatory, to find out why Rex always leaves unwelcome presents in the bathtub. Market yourself as a real Dr. Doolittle and you can make a killing.

☠ ☠ ☠   **$ $ $**   *tried it* ○

The Call of the Wild

655 **OPEN A PET CEMETERY.** Some people just can't stomach burying Fido in the backyard. Yet they still want to find a final resting place where they can visit at any time. Here's where you come in: make sure to charge a burial fee, maintenance fee, and a visiting fee. Just be sure it isn't over the site of a Native American burial ground. . . .

☠ ☠ ☠ $ $ *tried it* ○

656 **BECOME A PET TAXIDERMIST.** Crazy pet people want to hang on to their pets forever and, as pets become more like family members, there are fewer and fewer taxidermists agreeing to take this on. Fill this void in the market and grant these devoted pet owners their wish. With little competition, you'll be able to charge whatever you want. Find a taxidermy school near you at *www.learn-taxidermy.com/ taxidermy_schools.htm.*

☠ ☠ $ $ $ *tried it* ○

657 **FISH SIT.** You thought dog or cat sitting was easy! Trust me, there's nothing easier than fish sitting. Fish have to eat and need their water changed, and owners who are going away for any length of time, need to hire someone to watch over their aquatic pets. You many need to watch over the house as well, but there's nothing wrong with freeloading— as long as the fish are alive when their owners come home.

☠ $ *tried it* ○

658 **LEAD A SNORKELING GROUP.** Swimming with schools of fish in the Great Barrier Reef sounds more like a dream than a job, but add some school children to the mix and you can turn paradise into a lucrative career. Be sure to brush up on your jellyfish sting treatment and shark-avoidance strategies beforehand to prevent your snorkelers from becoming fish food.

☠ ☠ ☠ $ $ $ *tried it* ○

The Call of the Wild

659 **BREED FEEDER ANIMALS.** Where do you think the pet stores get those tiny mice you feed Butch, your boa constrictor? They don't just drop out of thin air; however, they are spawned for one particular purpose—Butch's supper. Talk to a local shop and see if you can under-price its feeder animal supplier.

☠ ☠ $ $ *tried it* ○

660 **SELL BAIT.** Worms are everywhere! They're just waiting unsuspecting in the dirt. Enter: you. If you're willing to get your hands dirty in the dirt, this is the perfect way to make a profit with no overhead. Really desperate? You can multiply your merchandise exponentially by chopping them in half.

☠ ☠ $ *tried it* ○

661 **CATCH AND SELL FISH.** With all of the news about how good omega-3 fatty acids are for you, it's a great time to catch and sell fish. Better yet, find some kids who love to fish and have them man the operation while you work the sales front.

☠ ☠ $ $ *tried it* ○

662 **LEAD A SCUBA TRIP.** You don't have to live in the tropics to get your scuba certification; many YMCAs or outdoor outfitters offer classes. Once you have your certification, plan a trip to the tropics—and charge others to let them come along.

☠ ☠ ☠ $ $ $ *tried it* ○

663 **GO CLAM DIGGING.** Who doesn't love being out in nature . . . very early in the morning . . . during low tide? Despite the smell—and the risk of the tide coming in on you—clamming allows you to rake in the clams (so to speak). Most states don't allow clamming without a license, so check out your state's Fish and Wildlife website for more info.

☠ ☠ ☠ $ $ *tried it* ○

664 **COLLECT MUSSELS.** Put on your galoshes and get ready to get down and dirty. Collecting mussels isn't easy, so try to find a local fisherman to give you some pointers. Also check local ordinances, as there are some places where it's illegal to mussel farm.

☠ ☠ $ $ $ *tried it* ○

665 **GO CRABBING.** If you've ever watched *Deadliest Catch* you know that crabbing isn't easy—but oh how they rake in the dough. And you don't necessarily have to move to Alaska to do it; just Google crabbing areas near you.

☠ ☠ ☠ ☠ $ $ $ $ *tried it* ○

666 **WORK AS A FARRIER.** There's more than one way to shoe a horse—or at least there is if you know how. Farriers are experts at dealing with horses' feet. They trim, clean, and shoe horses year round . . . and reap the rewards. Just be careful not to piss the horses off when you're that close to his feet. They pack quite a punch.

☠ ☠ ☠ $ $ $ *tried it* ○

The Call of the Wild

667 **JOCKEY.** Nothing beats the excitement of the track, especially if you're in the saddle. Because most jockeys are self-employed, the more races you win, the more money you can charge. Jockeying is a very lucrative career, but it's also very risky—jockeys are injured, debilitated, or killed every year.

☠ ☠ ☠ ☠ $ $ $ $ *tried it* ○

668 **GROOM HORSES.** Horses need to be groomed at least once a day, which means your working pretty consistently. Sounds a lot better than a nine-to-five job, right! Be careful though. Whenever you work with large animals, there's the risk of being kicked in the face. Go to *http://horses.about .com* to learn more.

☠ ☠ $ $ *tried it* ○

669 **FARM ALPACAS.** Have a big backyard? Fill it with moneymaking alpacas! The wool of the alpaca is highly prized—and highly priced. Every year, one alpaca will produce between five and ten pounds of soft wool that will sell for between two and five dollars per ounce. Talk about an investment! Go to *www.ilovealpacas.com/facts.shtml* for more info.

☠ ☠ $ $ $ *tried it* ○

670 **LEAD A MOUNTAIN-CLIMBING EXPEDITION.** Climb your way to the top by leading packs of adventure seekers in their quest for nice views, cool breezes, and the perfect handhold. Investing in the right equipment and training is key, but it can really pay off. In the off-season and in your down time you can run an indoor climbing gym so you're never sitting idly by.

☠ ☠ ☠ ☠ $ $ $ *tried it* ○

The Call of the Wild

671 **LEAD A SNOWSHOEING EXPEDITION.** No snowshoes? No problem! Just tie some tennis rackets to your feet! No but really. Snowshoeing is a great way to get around when there are inches of the fluffy white stuff coating the ground. It can also be a good way of seeing winter wildlife that would dash away at the sound of a snowmobile.

☠ ☠ ☠ $ $ $ *tried it* ○

672 **LEAD A CROSS-COUNTRY SKIING TRIP.** The other great way of seeing winter wildlife is on cross-country skis! Make sure that you know all of the signs of hypothermia and have a cell phone that stays within range; or make sure you have signed waivers from everyone attending saying that you're not responsible for frostbite or other cold-related illnesses.

☠ ☠ ☠ $ $ $ *tried it* ○

673 **WORK AS A SKI PATROLLER.** Okay, so being on the ski patrol isn't exactly *Baywatch*, but it serves a very necessary role on the slopes. And just think of the discounted lift tickets you'll get out of the deal! And the lives you'll save, of course.

☠ ☠ ☠ $ $ $ *tried it* ○

674 **FIND LOST PETS.** Channel your inner Ace Ventura and make the big bucks returning lost pets to desperate owners. You can scan local telephone poles for fliers or hit the Internet. Just make sure to only go for the ones that say "REWARD."

☠ ☠ $ $ *tried it* ○

675 **ENTER YOUR PET INTO CONTESTS.** Think your dog/cat/ pot-bellied pig is the cutest around? You may as well see if anyone else thinks the same thing and win some money at the same time. Pet shows range from the local country fair to the world-renowned Westminster Kennel Club dog show. The amount of money you can make depends on where you decide to show your pet.

☠ $ $ $ *tried it* ○

676 **WORK AS AN ANIMAL TRAINER.** Do you want to work with animals and break into the entertainment industry? Becoming an animal trainer will allow you to do both. Find training schools like the Hollywood Animals' Exotic Animal Training School (*www.animalschool.net*) online. Just be careful not to end up like Roy Horn of Siegfried and Roy.

☠ ☠ ☠ ☠ $ $ $ $ *tried it* ○

677 **BE A HIKE LEADER.** Hikes often sound good in theory. But when you're lost halfway up with no cell reception and it's getting dark, the fun turns to fear. Help the helpless go hiking by becoming a hike leader.

☠ ☠ $ $ *tried it* ○

678 **LEAD A CAMPING EXPEDITION.** Find people who would love to go camping but who don't have the will or the resources to purchase everything that goes along with it: tent, sleeping bags, sleeping pads, bug spray, portable stove. You can rent all of these items plus lead them to the best spots for camping and swimming. Charge extra to cook them meals.

☠ ☠ $ $ *tried it* ○

679	**BECOME AN OUTWARD BOUND INSTRUCTOR.** Could you stand to be in the wilderness for weeks at a time with teenagers? If you answered yes to this question then being an Outward Bound instructor is just the thing for you! You'll get to shape impressionable minds while teaching them how to dig a poop hole. Fun!

☠ ☠ ☠	$ $ $	*tried it* ○

680	**PAN FOR GOLD.** Where to find gold, where to find gold. . . . Enter *www.goldmaps.com*! Once you've picked your location, take the whole family along and get out your pan (a colander-like dish that let's you sift through material in water). Replace the gold the kids find with fool's gold and then sell it!

☠	$ $ $ $	*tried it* ○

681	**RUN A CAVE TOUR.** Are there some sick caves in your area? Go batty by running tours of them. These will be especially popular during the Halloween season if you advertise the bat aspect.

☠ ☠	$ $	*tried it* ○

682	**TAKE A GROUP SPELUNKING.** If your nearby caves run too vertical for cave walks, buy some harnesses and run spelunking expeditions. The cave episode of *Planet Earth* can give you some pointers on how to educate as you belay on.

☠ ☠ ☠	$ $ $	*tried it* ○

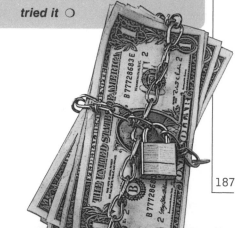

683 **LEAD A KAYAKING TRIP.** Wherever there is water, there is kayaking. Wherever there are fitness-minded tourists, there are people who want to go kayaking. It's the perfect combination! Consider moving somewhere like Alaska (but just for the summer of endless daylight) to be a kayak expedition leader.

☠ ☠ ☠ $ $ $ *tried it* ○

684 **LEAD A WHITEWATER RAFTING TRIP.** As bachelor parties and male bonding trips start to take it to the extreme rather than to the strip clubs, excursions like whitewater rafting have become more in-demand. Put your paddling and leadership skills to use and charge to take groups down the rapids.

☠ ☠ ☠ $ $ $ *tried it* ○

685 **BECOME A WRANGLER.** We're all familiar with that iconic image of the cowboy wrangling cattle out on the open plain, but it may surprise you to realize that that image isn't just one from the past. Many ranches—both for tourists and cattle production—are still hiring wranglers today. So grab your chaps and lasso and find your home on the range. Go to *www.ranchwork.com* to see what's out there.

☠ $ $ $ *tried it* ○

686 **FARM EMUS.** You wouldn't think that there was a big market for the emu in the United States, but due to the adaptability of these big birds, farms are popping up all over the country. Emus don't take up a lot of room compared to other types of livestock and have been called "the totally usable bird" because the full animal (meat, claws, oil, feathers, etc.) can be used and sold.

☠ ☠ $ $ $ *tried it* ○

687 **RUN A TURKEY FARM.** The average American eats 18 pounds of turkey a year. Take advantage of this diet staple by starting your own turkey farm. Sure, turkeys are dirty and mean birds, but you'll never have to wait in line at the deli.

☠ $ $ $ *tried it* ○

688 **SELL STEW RABBITS.** A good rabbit stew is a staple of down-home Southern cooking. As long as you can separate emotional attachment from financial gain, you should have no problem putting Thumper and friends up for sale.

☠ $ $ *tried it* ○

689 **KEEP BEES AND SELL HONEY.** Honey bees are becoming a hot commodity, so do your part for your wallet and the future of all things sweet by becoming a bee keeper. Remember, scarcity drives up prices, so make sure to tell your customers to get their honey while they still can —before all of the honey bees disappear and we have robotic bees pollinating flowers.

☠ ☠ ☠ $ $ $ *tried it* ○

690 **SHEAR SHEEP.** How hard can it be? Most sheep are sheared with electric shearers. It's just like using an electric razor on your face. Most small sheep farmers have trouble finding a shearer to come out to their property and usually have to pay to bring their sheep to a central location. This is expensive for the farmers, and you can capitalize on this by putting some of that money in your own pocket. Sheep are sheared twice a year, which means you earn a fairly steady income.

☠ $ $ $ *tried it* ○

691 RAISE CHICKENS. Cock-a-doodle do this! Keeping chickens offers many opportunities for making money, and you can do it in your own backyard. You can sell eggs, rent out roosters as alarm clocks, and cut down on dinner costs (sorry chickens). BackyardChickens (*www.backyardchickens.com*) tells you everything you need to know to get your flock started.

☠ $ $ *tried it* ○

692 RAISE COWS AND SELL MILK. You don't have to buy fifty or even five cows to make some money selling milk. Everyone is into organic, local, natural food products today, and you can capitalize on this by selling close to home. Be careful, though, even one cow takes up a lot of room, and milk needs to be pasteurized before it can be sold in most states.

☠ ☠ ☠ $ $ $ *tried it* ○

693 RAISE PIGS AND SELL MEAT. One little piggy went to market, and one little piggy went wee-wee-wee all the way to the bank. Pot-bellied pig owners would disagree, but raising pigs for the butcher can be a good way to earn money. Contrary to popular belief, pigs aren't that smelly, they don't take up a lot of space, and you can sell their waste as fertilizer. It's a win-win situation . . . unless you're the pig.

☠ $ $ $ *tried it* ○

694 HOCK HOGS FOR LUAUS. There's a difference between selling a pig for pork chops and putting one up for sale for a pig roast. First of all, there's no cutting involved on your part. The person looking to throw a luau wants the pig, the whole pig, and nothing but the pig. You could make some additional money, though, by offering your post-roasting chopping skills. No host wants to mingle with his guests after slicing and de-boning their dinner.

☠ $ $ *tried it* ○

695 **GIVE BIGFOOT TOURS.** People are looking for more than a walk in the woods nowadays. Market yourself as a Sasquatch specialist and take amateur monster hunters out for a hike to remember. You can increase your notoriety by having a friend stalk around in an altered ape suit. Just be sure you're not leading any overzealous adventurers who are packing heat.

☠ ☠ ☠ $ $ *tried it* ○

696 **LEAD A WALKABOUT.** An Aboriginal rite of passage, the walkabout is meant as a journey of spiritual enlightenment. You don't need to take those who have enrolled all the way to the Outback, but you should find a place that's far removed from any notion of civilization.

☠ ☠ $ $ $ *tried it* ○

CHAPTER 12

Get Your Hands Dirty

Skilled labor will always be in demand. Maybe it's time to lose the bookworm habits, roll up your sleeves, and enter one of the many trades to make some money. A little elbow grease never hurt anyone.

697 **MEND CLOTHES.** When times are tough, people would rather fix what they have than buy new clothes. If you're skilled at wielding a needle and thread, put your skills as a tailor up for sale. Neighborhood cleaners are probably willing to let you advertise in their shops.

⚒ $ *tried it* ○

698 **COBBLE SHOES.** You don't have to be an elf. Fixing shoes is a valuable skill, and once the word gets around, you'll never want for business. Just don't start dressing in green and smoking a pipe.

⚒ $ *tried it* ○

699 **WORK AS A TAILOR.** You've been taking in (and letting out) your own suits since you started your 9-to-5 working for the man. Turn your tailor skills into a moneymaking opportunity. Plenty of people will be trying to squeeze into their old suits for interviews after a long layoff binge.

⚒ ⚒ $ $ *tried it* ○

700 **CHOP WOOD AND SELL IT AS FIREWOOD.** If there are trees on your property—especially ones with big fallen branches—you may be looking at an income source. Cut up the wood into logs with a chainsaw and then split it, either with an axe or, if you've got the money to invest, a log-splitter.

⚒ ⚒ $ *tried it* ○

701 **START A LANDSCAPING BUSINESS.** You'll need the basic tools (shovel, rake, pitchfork, wheelbarrow), a business card, and a lot of elbow grease. This is a great job to take up in the spring when homeowners want their houses looking their best. Pick up a couple of books on landscape design at the local library.

⚒ $ $ $ *tried it* ○

702 **PLASTER SOMEONE'S WALL.** It's simpler than it looks, and these days there's a ton of videos available over the Web on how to repair a damaged wall. The tools you'll need are at the local hardware store. An ad in your community newspaper will get you your first couple of jobs.

☠   *$ $*   *tried it* ○

703 **INSTALL A GREEN ROOF.** Everyone's going green these days. One of the first ways to green a house is to put in solar panels. You don't need an engineering degree—just the ability to follow instructions on mounting the panels. Check out some different sites online so you can offer your customers competitive prices for purchase and installation.

☠   *$ $ $*   *tried it* ○

704 **SAND AND REFINISH A FLOOR.** For a small fee, you can rent one of those big floor sanders. Once you build up enough cash, invest in one of your own. This kind of work builds by word of mouth, so be sure to ask your first customers to tell all their friends what a great job you did.

☠   *$ $*   *tried it* ○

705 **WINTER-PROOF SOMEONE'S HOUSE.** With winters turning colder, no one wants to lose energy through cracks in windows or faulty insulation. Offer your services to make sure people stay warm and dry and save on energy costs. It's another green business your customers will appreciate.

☠   *$ $*   *tried it* ○

Get Your Hands Dirty

706 **POST A FENCE.** "Good fences make good neighbors." That's what a lot of people think. Get a posthole digger, a shovel, and a pair of sturdy work gloves and you're set to go as the neighborhood's number one fence builder. Whether it's wire, wood, or white picket, you'll be there.

☠ $ $ *tried it* ○

707 **PAINT A FENCE.** Okay, you put up a fence. (Or someone else did.) But it's going to need a coat of paint to protect it from the elements and make it (and the house it goes with) look good. You're there to leap into a pair of coveralls, pick up a paintbrush or sprayer, and get to work.

☠ $ *tried it* ○

708 **TAKE DOWN A FENCE.** Maybe it's falling down. Maybe it's blocking a great view. Maybe your customers just plain don't like fences. Whatever the case, they'll pay to have you pull it out of the ground and haul it away. A long, thin spade and a pickup truck are the tools you'll need here.

☠ $ $ *tried it* ○

709 **BUILD A RETAINING WALL.** Did you know that Winston Churchill used to relax by building walls? That's right. Of course, you can and should get paid for it. If you like messing around with bricks or stones, mortar, and a trowel and level, this is a source of relaxation and profit.

☠ ☠ $ $ *tried it* ○

710 **DETAIL A CAR.** It's true that this takes a bit of specialized knowledge. If you've never detailed a car before, you probably don't want to experiment on your neighbor's Porsche. But if you know how to properly detail a car and have an artistic feeling that you want to express, this could be the job for you. And if you want to learn, sign up for a class at your local community college.

☠ $ $ *tried it* ○

711 **LAY A PATIO.** Lots of homeowners want a nice, quiet place with a barbecue grill where they can relax at the end of the day. Offer your services. You'll need a shovel, a level, and a strong back for carrying bricks and stones. It doesn't hurt to have an artistic eye so you can create attractive patterns on the patio. Customers will pay extra for that.

☠ ☠   *$ $ $*   *tried it* ○

712 **BUILD A DECK.** Those people who don't want a patio probably want a deck. There are a ton of books about how to build anything from a simple platform to an elaborate three-story masterpiece. A miter saw is a helpful piece of equipment for this line of work, as well as a nail gun.

☠   *$ $ $*   *tried it* ○

713 **CLEAN GUTTERS.** When winter's ending and spring's just around the corner, people start to clean out the leaves and dead branches from their roof gutters. Well, actually, they hire someone to do it. And that someone could be you. It's simple and just involves standing on a ladder or climbing on a roof for a while.

☠   *$*   *tried it* ○

714 **CUT DOWN A TREE.** Want to be Paul Bunyan? Of course, you don't have to do it with an axe (or a big blue ox). These days a chainsaw is the preferred tool. This can be a bit risky—you have to be sure not to hit anything or anyone with the falling tree. This might be a good job to go into business with your uncle, father, nephew, or neighbor.

☠ ☠ ☠   *$ $ $*   *tried it* ○

715 **REMOVE A STUMP.** Big trees have deep roots. They take a lot of digging to get out of the ground. If you're up for it, a stump removal service could meet a big need in the area where you live. If you make enough money at it, you can even invest in a stump grinder, which makes the process faster (and louder).

      $ $ *tried it* ○

716 **INSTALL A POND.** You can dig a hole in the ground and line it with plastic, surrounded by rocks. Or you can go whole hog and have a multilevel pond with goldfish and a solar-powered fountain in the middle. Either way, you can charge people to install it. A pond adds beauty to any property, and it can add bucks to your wallet.

      $ $ $ *tried it* ○

717 **WATERSCAPE.** After a successful pond installation, most homeowners will want to create a picturesque scene in their man-made body of water. If you have the skills to install and style, offer a deal on a two-for. Try to capture the overall feel they want using fish, stones, and water plants.

      $ $ *tried it* ○

718 **PAVE A DRIVEWAY.** If you have access to some heavy equipment, you can lay down a crushed gravel driveway or even, if you're ambitious and know what you're doing, an asphalt one. Just be careful and make sure you've got all the right permits and insurance.

     $ $ $ *tried it* ○

Get Your Hands Dirty

719 RESEED A LAWN. The best time for lawn maintenance jobs like this is in the early fall or early spring. Everyone wants his or her lawn to look its best when the days get warmer and the grass is green, lush, and evenly cut. Your basic investment is in the grass seed and a spreader.

☠ $ $ *tried it* ○

720 FIX A GARBAGE DISPOSAL. Aside from toilets, this is the household appliance that probably breaks down most often (possibly from the little kid who tries to stick his sister's Barbie doll down it). Got a mechanical turn of mind? Don't mind messing with other people's garbage? Put an ad up on craigslist and see what happens.

☠ ☠ $ *tried it* ○

721 INSTALL A GARBAGE DISPOSAL. This is a simple, basic home improvement that lots of people want but don't know how to do. The instructions that come with the disposal unit should tell you the basics of how to do it. Check online for any tips and tricks that will save you time and money.

☠ $ $ *tried it* ○

722 REFACE KITCHEN CABINETS. Think about it: Those people who want to sell their homes in a down market don't have the money to pay a company to make their home look better. That's where you come in with your affordable, reasonable offer to give their kitchens a face-lift.

☠ $ $ *tried it* ○

723 RESHINGLE A ROOF. You really are starting to look pale these days. Get a tan and earn some money by climbing on some roofs and shingling like there is no tomorrow. Dumping the old shingles can be a pain though, so make sure you have a plan on how to dispose of them—and be sure to factor any disposal fees into your job estimate.

☠ ☠ ☠ $ $ $ *tried it* ○

724 **PAINT THE EXTERIOR OF A HOUSE.** Homeowners always want to be proud of their investment—in good times and in bad. However, there's no way in hell they can feel proud if people can see paint chipping around their windows. Offer to slap a brand-new coat of paint on (after spending hours scraping the old layer off, of course).

☠ ☠ $ $ $ *tried it* ○

725 **PAINT THE INTERIOR OF A HOUSE.** Casually tell your friends that the paint job in their home looks like monkeys threw feces at the walls, and you would be happy to repaint for a price. If your tactful attempts to get hired by your buddies don't pan out, placing ads on craigslist works too.

☠ $ $ *tried it* ○

726 **BE A CARPENTER'S APPRENTICE.** You were able to build that bookshelf with minimal injury, so why not try full-fledged carpentry? The woodworking art covers a wide range of products created and services rendered. Find a licensed carpenter and see if he needs a hand. This answers the age-old question, what would Jesus do (in a financial crunch)?

☠ ☠ $ $ *tried it* ○

727 **WORK AS AN ELECTRICIAN'S APPRENTICE.** You're the person everybody turns to for advice about electric installations—even though you don't have that whole "license" thing figured out yet. Save yourself an expensive lawsuit and go legit. Ask an area electrician to be your Obi-wan. For more enlightening information, try this site: *www .njatc.org*.

☠ ☠ ☠ $ $ $ *tried it* ○

728 **WORK AS A LATE-NIGHT MAINTENANCE ENGINEER.** This isn't much different than when you clean your own house, except you'll get paid. You'll find these types of gigs at local schools and businesses by checking the classifieds, scouring job listings on bulletin boards, and asking the places' human resources departments about openings.

☠ $ $ *tried it* ○

729 **REPAIR WOOL CLOTHES.** Take out your kit and start offering to patch things up. The clientele is a lot larger than you think—preppies and hipsters alike sport wool sweaters. And they're just as likely to be the victims of tears and moths.

☠ $ *tried it* ○

730 **WEAVE YARN.** Knitting has become the trendy thing to do as of late. Capitalize on the growth of this crafty hobby by weaving and selling your own yarn. These home-hobbyists will appreciate handmade material.

☠ $ *tried it* ○

731 **SIDE A HOUSE.** This is a little different than just painting a house. (And by a *little*, we mean a *lot*.) However, if you know what you're doing—go for it. You'll need to stock up on supplies, so make sure your estimation skills are in good working order before you go out offering your services.

☠ ☠ ☠ $ $ $ *tried it* ○

732 **CHANGE OTHERS' OIL.** If swapping out old oil is something that comes easy to you, charge others for a driveway fill-up. Make sure you tell them how difficult and strenuous it is, so they'll keep coming back to you.

☠ $ $ *tried it* ○

733 **DO CAR TUNE-UPS.** If you're really car savvy, you can start offering tune-ups. Undercut the area competition and offer these tune-ups on craigslist and to your friends. Watch out, though—if your car breaks down and you need a real mechanic, he might not take too kindly to the guy who stole his business.

☠ ☠ $ $ *tried it* ○

734 **REPLACE BRAKE PADS.** Brakes are beautiful things. They slow you down, bring you to a stop, and save your life. But most people treat their brakes like trash—stomping on them to come to a screeching halt. That's why brake pads are replaced so often, and if you know how to do this swapout, you can start charging friends for service with a smile. Along with taking care of oil changes and car tune-ups, eventually you'll be running an almost-legitimate garage.

☠ ☠ $ $ *tried it* ○

735 **SWEEP CHIMNEYS FOR CASH.** Chimney sweeping isn't your great-great-great grandfather's business anymore. You can use tools that weren't available back in the Victorian-era to clean modern-day heating appliances. In addition to making some cash, you'll also increase your chances of being on Santa Claus's nice list. See the National Chimney Sweep Guild (*www.ncsg.org*) for more information.

☠ ☠ $ $ *tried it* ○

736 **INSTALL NEW WINDOWS.** You hired a company to install your windows, and it didn't look that hard (they were sitting around half the time anyway). You can offer to do this for a much lower price. Just be careful that you measure everything correctly or else you'll have furious customers and get caught footing the bill for the professionals to fix your mistakes.

☠ ☠ ☠ $ $ $ *tried it* ○

737 **INSTALL ENERGY-EFFICIENT LIGHT BULBS.** Green is still in, especially since Obama got into office. Go around your neighborhood and ask your neighbors if they would be interested in light bulbs that will save them money (while you charge a modest fee).

☠ $ *tried it* ○

738 **CLEAN OUT FIREPLACES.** It's a messy, dirty job, but someone has to do it, and that someone is *you*. You will financially benefit from residents wanting a working fireplace that doesn't cause them to become sick. Make sure you wear protective gear to fight off the dust and debris.

☠ ☠ $ $ *tried it* ○

739 **REPAIR DENTS IN CARS.** Anyone who's ever fixed a ding without taking their car in and getting into a financial collision with their mechanic can hire out as a dent-fixer. Don't divulge your secrets to your dented clientele (be it canned air, dry ice, or a hair dryer). You wouldn't want them doing this on their own.

☠ $ $ *tried it* ○

Get Your Hands Dirty

740 **TILE A BATHROOM.** You've done your business in enough disgusting bathrooms in others' homes and at the local bars (think *Trainspotting*'s "the worst bathroom in the world") to know just about everyone's could use some fixing up. While a fresh set of tiles won't completely wipe away any lingering scents, you could earn yourself some dollars turning these literal crap holes into cleaner places.

☠ ☠ $ $ $ *tried it* ○

741 **UNCLOG SHOWER AND SINK DRAINS.** You've worked enough bottle caps and lime rinds out of your sink to know what's up when the water won't go down. And your skills at plucking hair-dolls out of the shower drain are surpassed by none. Therefore, you should take your show on the road. Put up ads on college campuses (those kids get all sorts of stuff stuck in their drains) and on craigslist offering your service. *Hopefully*, it's just hair down there.

☠ $ $ *tried it* ○

742 **TOW CARS.** Be the AAA-alternative and offer to get your tow on for a reasonable price. Whether you actually own a tow truck (what the hell are you doing with a tow truck?) or are just able to hitch broken-down rides to yours, you can make some serious cash from others' distress and distrust of companies that financially rape by the mile.

☠ ☠ $ $ $ *tried it* ○

743 **HITCH UP OTHERS' BOATS.** You've had to sell your boat to pay off your debts, but don't worry, Skipper, you can still use that towing equipment to your advantage. Put up fliers at local marinas and post ads on craigslist that offer your services. Just be sure to factor in gas prices when you figure out your fee.

☠ $ $ *tried it* ○

744 **WINTERIZE BOATS.** Boats are lots of fun in the summer when it's warm out and you're all carefree bopping around the lake or river. But when winter rolls in it's no fun having to pull the boat out of the water. Do this for people for a fee—make some extra cash by also storing it for the winter (you don't need that extra space in your backyard, right?).

☠ ☠ $ $ *tried it* ○

745 **PLOW SNOW.** If you have an SUV with four-wheel drive, it might be to your financial benefit to check out eBay for a used plow to hitch to your vehicle. While there's some up-front cost associated with this entry, following through and starting your own plow service will make you enough to pay your month's oil bill in only a few hours.

☠ $ $ $ *tried it* ○

746 **RE-LAY A WALKWAY.** Pulling up bricks and slate, tamping down soil, and laying new stones in the summer heat—what better way to spend a Saturday? Offer to fix up your friends' and neighbors' walkways for a price. Just make sure that price includes the materials needed if they expect you to purchase them.

☠ $ $ *tried it* ○

747 **INSTALL DOOR LOCKS.** Cut newspaper clippings or pass on stories (either true and fabricated) to your neighbors about recent home invasions where the intruders were able to enter because of weak locks. Then tell them how you learned to install reinforced locking mechanisms in your spare time. You'll basically be robbing them of their money.

☠   **$**   *tried it* ○

748 **PUT IN NEW DOORS.** Forget installing new locks. Why not go for the whole shebang and offer to put in a brand new door? Maybe customers want more security, or possibly a change in the exterior look of their house—whatever the case, you can score some sweet change by changing the way they enter their home.

☠   **$ $**   *tried it* ○

749 **INSTALL WATER HEATERS.** Nobody likes taking a cold shower—unless of course you *need* one. Heat things up by being the only water heater install-person in your neighborhood. Who knows, maybe you'll meet some homeowners who will make you want a cold shower.

☠ ☠   **$ $**   *tried it* ○

750 **INSTALL KITCHEN APPLIANCES.** Some people trying to save a buck will opt to go without the installation fee that comes with buying a new appliance and attempt to do it themselves. (A smaller fraction of new-appliance owners will waive a free installation thinking they can do it themselves.) Chances are—in both cases—they will fail. Luckily for them, you know what you're doing, and will do it for a price.

☠   **$ $ $**   *tried it* ○

751 **WALLPAPER.** Grab a ladder, it's time to hang some wallpaper. Transform a nursery into a Disney wonderland or a bathroom into a Monet painting. Think you're really pretty good at this whole wallpapering thing? Grab your camcorder and make a video of yourself doing it (see entry 752).

☠ ☠ $ $ *tried it* ○

752 **SELL AN INSTRUCTIONAL VIDEO.** Did you discover when making money off of one of these ideas that you're actually extremely good at it? So good, in fact, that you should be teaching other people? Film yourself giving step-by-step instructions and see if you can find any takers. You can always sign up to be an About.com guide, where you get paid to post blogs and videos about a specific topic.

☠ ☠ $ $ *tried it* ○

753 **BE AN ON-CALL HANDYMAN.** If you're not picky about getting woken up in the middle of the night when people realize that their [fill in the blank] is broken, you can make good money as an on-call handyman. Make sure people know that you're available twenty-four hours a day, and charge them to reflect that.

☠ ☠ ☠ $ $ $ *tried it* ○

754 **BE A "HUSBAND-FOR-HIRE."** It may sound sexist, but a husband-for-hire is exactly what some women are looking for: a couple of dedicated man-hours with no need to clean up after them (or listen to them complain about doing the work). Even married women will be lining up to pay you to service them—er, their homes, that is.

☠ ☠ $ $ $ *tried it* ○

755 **POWERWASH SIDING.** Because a somewhat large machine is needed for this job, you can earn back your investment by purchasing one—especially if you're the only game in town and there are lots of houses with vinyl siding.

☠ ☠ $ $ $ *tried it* ○

756 **SANDBLAST PATIOS AND WALKWAYS.** Thinking that a sandblaster is too expensive for you? Consider sharing the cost—and the use—of a sandblaster with a couple of friends. This works especially well if you live in different areas of a city so that you can each corner your own market.

☠ ☠ $ $ $ *tried it* ○

757 **EXTERMINATE RODENTS AND BUGS.** Live out your childhood fantasy of being a ghost buster by becoming an exterminator. People want pests gone so badly they likely won't say a word about you walking through the house singing "Who you gonna call?"

☠ ☠ ☠ $ $ $ *tried it* ○

758 **FIX BIKES.** Gas prices are all over the map these days, causing more people to bike to work. Advertise yourself in well-populated office buildings; you can fix several bikes per day and have an "in by 9 ready by 5 policy."

☠ ☠ $ $ *tried it* ○

759 **CONVERT A HOME FROM OIL TO GAS.** Gas is cleaner and cheaper than oil (which has to be delivered—it just seems so milkman ancient). Making the switch over is tricky business, though, so make sure you know what you're doing. Gas might burn cleaner, but neither gas nor oil is something people want leaking.

☠ ☠ ☠ $ $ $ *tried it* ○

760 **CONVERT A HOME FROM GAS TO ELECTRIC.** Even cleaner than gas, electric heat is the ultimate in green heating. Help wanna-be environmentalists convert their house from gas to electric. When you're done, you can help them go paperless (see entry 301) and cut down on electricity use (see entry 761).

☠ ☠ ☠ $ $ $ *tried it* ○

761 **FIX UP PEOPLE'S HOMES TO REDUCE ELECTRIC BILLS.** Put timers on lights, replace old bulbs with energy-efficient ones, and counsel people on their electronics use. For example, does that DVD player need to be plugged in and ready to go 24/7? I thought not.

☠ $ $ *tried it* ○

762 **REWIRE SOMEONE'S HOUSE.** This is great for people who purchased a "fixer-upper" and aren't so much into the "fixing" aspect, especially when it comes to the wiring. All those high-tech gadgets need to be charged somewhere, even in extremely old houses that were built before the dawn of the iPod.

☠ ☠ ☠ $ $ $ $ *tried it* ○

Get Your Hands Dirty

763 **CONVERT A CELLAR OR ATTIC INTO A NEW ROOM.** Did your friend mention wanting to rent out an extra room or turn a basement room into a darkroom to rent out? (Wonder where he got those ideas . . .) Make these spaces livable by putting your carpentry and plumbing skills to the test.

☠ ☠ $ $ $ *tried it* ○

764 **WAX PEOPLE'S SURFBOARDS.** Wax is an important part of surfing and if not done correctly can make a surfer look more like shark bait. Not sure what kind to use? Want to learn more about waxing in general? Take a trip to the Surf Wax Museum at *www.surfwaxmuseum.com*.

☠ $ *tried it* ○

765 **TUNE SKIS.** Put your master waxing skills to good use by sharpening and smoothing skiers' equipment pre-season. Other people's Atomics aren't something to mess around with, though. Know what you're doing before you go offering out your services. Forgetting your melting iron on the bottom of a ski, or messing with someone's edge, is a double-black level risk.

☠ ☠ $ *tried it* ○

766 **REPAIR SOLAR PANELS.** As more and more people are going green for resource preservation and wallet padding, there will be a greater need for people who know how to fix these new technologies. Get a handle on solar panel maintenance and you'll be able to charge a good price since there's relatively few competitors.

☠ ☠ $ $ $ *tried it* ○

767 **BUILD A WINDMILL.** Sunlight's not the only thing in nature that's free and can make you money—so can wind! Build windmills for people who want to harness the natural energy of the wind. To find out how, visit *www.makeyour ownwindmill.net.*

☠ ☠ *$ $ $* *tried it* ○

768 **INSULATE A HOME.** Screw global warming; the winter is still colder than a witch's you know what. Help people keep warm next winter by charging them to insulate their home. Remind them that they'll save money on heating costs, so while your fee might seem huge at the moment they're really saving money in the long run.

☠ *$ $* *tried it* ○

769 **DO DESERT LANDSCAPING.** It's obviously harder to land-scape in a place that doesn't get much water than it is in a moisture-rich climate. That's where you come in—with your "expert" desert landscaping skills. Make sure to read up about cacti first.

☠ ☠ *$ $* *tried it* ○

770 **BALE HAY.** Hay comes in bales—but it doesn't put itself into those uniform sizes. You'll develop some great pipes, get a tan, and have girls screaming for your cowboyesque nature. Check with local farms to see who needs help.

☠ *$ $* *tried it* ○

771 **ENTER A TRACTOR PULL.** Are you and your John Deere a force to be reckoned with? Show everyone else you mean business and enter the annual tractor pull at your local fair. You could land yourself a blue ribbon and some green bills (or some equipment that you can hock online to put you back in the black).

☠ *$ $* *tried it* ○

772 **INSTALL CAR SOUND SYSTEMS.** Car stereos tend to scare people; they think they'll connect the wrong wire in the wrong place and end up with a $1,000 dashboard decoration that doesn't work. Put your skills to use by getting the car owners who want to skirt the cost of having it installed at Sears to take out the middleman and pay you to do it.

☠ ☠　　　　$ $　　　*tried it* ○

773 **DO POST-FACTORY CAR INSTALLATIONS.** Not everyone can afford to buy a car that comes complete with all the bells and whistles—like a car-starter or an alarm system. If you possess the skills to pimp someone's ride, advertise yourself as such on sites like craigslist.

☠ ☠　　　　$ $ $　　　*tried it* ○

774 **BECOME A LOCKSMITH.** To become a locksmith you need to take a class and then pass the locksmithing certification test. If that sounds like a good time to you, it's time to become a locksmith. And with all of the interesting people you open doors for, you'll have lots of fodder for your locksmithing memoir!

☠ ☠　　　　$ $　　　*tried it* ○

775 **PICK CORN.** Corn gets "knee high by the Fourth of July" so plan on cashing in around August. As more industries begin to rely on corn (corn syrup, corn-fed beef, corn-based biodegradable forks, etc.) the need for people to pick it also grows.

☠ ☠ $ *tried it* ○

776 **PICK COTTON.** Picking cotton is not for the faint of heart. Waking up in the middle of the night and working through the heat of the day can be hard, but if you live in a prime cotton-growing area this is a fast way to make some cash.

☠ ☠ ☠ $ *tried it* ○

777 **PICK SUMMER CROPS.** This is a great summer job for teachers who have nothing else to do. Why not pick some fruit in your off time? Manual labor will tone your muscles and give you a great tan that your students will envy come fall.

☠ ☠ $ $ *tried it* ○

778 **HARVEST AND SELL TOBACCO.** Use your green thumb to feed other people's addiction to nicotine (called such due to the Nicotiana plant) by growing and selling tobacco. This works best in sunny warm climates (like the South) and in areas where smoking is still legal inside (like the South).

☠ ☠ ☠ $ $ $ *tried it* ○

779 **GROW A PUMPKIN PATCH.** Put that extra space in your backyard to good use by planting some pumpkin seeds. When the fall rolls around, you can sell pumpkins, run a haunted house (see entry 59), and run a corn maze (see entry 640)!

☠ $ $ *tried it* ○

780 **RUN A CHRISTMAS TREE FARM.** If you want to make money from a Christmas tree farm, start now—you'll reap the rewards in around four to fifteen years. For instant gratification, cut down the existing trees in your yard or buy some land that's populated with spruces.

☠ ☠ $ $ $ *tried it* ○

781 **SELL FLOWERS FROM YOUR GARDEN.** It's nice to look out at your garden full of beautiful, colorful flowers. But it's even nicer to have cash, so start clipping. Get some cheap vases and ribbon and charge extra for packaging.

☠ ☠ $ $ *tried it* ○

782 **GROW AND SELL HEMP.** Believe it or not, it's actually legal to grow hemp (which comes from the cannabis plant) in the United States. That is, of course, if you have a permit from the Drug Enforcement Administration. For more information visit *www.industrialhemp.net.*

☠ ☠ $ $ $ *tried it* ○

783 **GET A LICENSE TO SELL MEDICAL MARIJUANA.** Thirteen states currently allow the use of medical marijuana, but make sure you check all the rules and regulations of your state before you apply for a license. If you get one, you can grow a certain number of plants and sell it to those who have a license to use medical marijuana. The details are different for every state, so be sure to do your research!

☠ ☠ ☠ ☠ $ $ $ *tried it* ○

784 **CONDUCT SEPTIC TANK MAINTENANCE.** For those who have sewer access, you might not be familiar with septic tanks. Septics are systems usually located underground that hold and break down household waste. However, some "waste" isn't easily broken down, and often results in issues for the homeowner. Therefore, if you understand how a septic works—and what needs to be done when it isn't working—you can become a septic repairman. Either post your services online, or look for distressed owners looking to get their systems fixed.

☠ ☠ $ $ $ *tried it* ○

785 **DIG A WELL.** Putting in a well is no simple task. First of all there needs to be a water source to tap into. Secondly, you need the knowledge and equipment to complete the task. If there is a source to tap, you know how to do it, and have what you need—go for it. The risk is high, but the payoff is higher for a successful well installation.

☠ ☠ ☠ $ $ $ $ *tried it* ○

786 **INSTALL AN IRRIGATION SYSTEM.** Depending on how extensive the system is, you could charge a lot of money for the digging and piping of an irrigation system. Even if it's only meant to cater to a single household's lawn and garden watering, a well-dug and -placed system will set any homeowner back a pretty penny—which will end up in your pocket.

☠ ☠ $ $ $ *tried it* ○

787 **RE-UPHOLSTER FURNITURE.** You can save others the hassle (and expense) of going out and buying a new set of sofas and chairs if you can flawlessly upholster their existing furniture. Let them choose the material, color, and pattern of their liking and then add the expense of the material needed with your labor charges.

☠ $ $ *tried it* ○

788 **BUILD AN OUTDOOR FIREPLACE.** Backyards are becoming the new place to impress friends and family with well-designed layouts and all the necessary toys. One outdoor addition that's an absolute must is the outdoor fireplace. If you know how to lay brick and can build a structure capable of sustaining heat, the sky's the limit in terms of design and how much you can charge for an intricately designed outside oven.

☠ ☠ $ $ $ *tried it* ○

789 **PUT UP SHUTTERS.** You should see if the homeowner wants to complement their new windows with sets of shutters. Whether they're meant to be a dressing or functional, shutter installation can net you some nice money. Just don't fall off your ladder.

☠ ☠ $ $ *tried it* ○

790 **MOUNT MOLDING.** One way to alter the interior aesthetic of a home is by installing molding. The beveling and contours provided by molding can give a room dramatic depth and height. However, these wooden pieces aren't easy to install. If you have the necessary know-how, you can capitalize on the DIY interior decorator who doesn't *really* have the DIY part down.

☠ ☠ $ $ *tried it* ○

CHAPTER 13

Wired Up

Now that geek has become chic, you can come out of the computer-skill closet—and cash in on the fact that your pantheon of heroes includes Bill Gates and Steve Jobs. Help others step up to Web 2.0 and pad your wallet in the process—*w00t*!

791 **OPEN A SECOND LIFE BOUTIQUE.** Virtual worlds come with virtual money and virtual consumers. All you have to do is cash in on that virtual demand. Reebok, American Apparel, and Armani have all jumped into the retail 2.0 game. Now it's your chance to set up a niche shop, develop some wild skins, and roll in Linden dollars (the Second Life currency).

☠   **$ $**   *tried it* ○

792 **DEVELOP SECOND LIFE REAL ESTATE.** This is one real estate market Trump has not gotten his hands on—*yet.* Your best bet is to sign up for a premium account ($9.95 a month), which starts you with a plot of land as well as a weekly stipend of 300 Linden dollars, and start building your empire. If you have a knack for e-architecture and design, you should be good. If you don't, the virtual world needs e-hookers too.

☠ ☠   **$ $ $**   *tried it* ○

793 **MINE AND SELL *WARCRAFT* GOLD.** Gamers with dealings in *World of Warcraft* know that the currency to use is gold coins—and that these e-pieces can fetch a good real world price. If you're down to "grind for gold," you can turn your mining skills into actual money.

☠ ☠   **$ $**   *tried it* ○

794 **HOCK YOUR GAMING HERO.** It takes a lot of effort and a lot of time to build up the skill levels of characters in massively multiplayer online role-playing games like *World of Warcraft.* However, if you're good enough—and quick enough—you can crank out super-skilled heroes to sell to other not-so-good gamers. Just beware, e-hero trafficking isn't allowed in some games' user agreements.

☠ ☠ ☠   **$ $ $**   *tried it* ○

795 **TUTOR GAMERS.** Help the less-talented newbs by giving insight on how to rule online worlds. Become the virtual Mr. Miyagi to their e-grasshoppers. Set up a PayPal account and host sessions showing them the ins and outs of owning other joystick junkies.

☠   *$ $*   *tried it* ○

796 **TAKE A FALL IN A VIDEO GAME—FOR MONEY.** What better way for a newbie to show he's mastered the art than to have him take down his sensei? Of course, there's no way he could *really* beat you (we hope). But as long as his credit card clears, it's time to let him fake it in front of his gaming friends. Beware though, your credibility may take a nosedive if one too many Daniel-sans take you down.

☠ ☠   *$ $*   *tried it* ○

797 **TEACH GAMERS HOW TO CHEAT.** Those who can, do; those who can't, *cheat*. All games have certain bugs or hacks that you can exploit. The hard part isn't finding out *how* to cheat, it's figuring out how to cheat without getting caught. Your mission, if you choose to accept it, is to train amateur con artists how to get away with whupping some ass illegally. (Only accept if you don't mind risking your online rep.)

☠ ☠ ☠   *$ $*   *tried it* ○

798 **WRITE GAMING GUIDES.** If you're good—and we mean *real* good—and you're fast—and we mean *real* fast—you could go into business cranking out companion texts to the newest video games. The only problem is you need to be able to beat the game in a short amount of time and crank out your guide to make sure it's out when the game's still relevant. If you think you have what it takes, try soliciting the two official strategy guide publishers: Prima Games and BradyGames. Just don't plan on having a life.

☠ ☠   *$ $*   *tried it* ○

799 **BECOME A GAME TESTER.** Speaking of lives, this is *it*: Sitting on your couch, scarfing junk food, going full-throttle on a game that hasn't even hit store shelves yet—and calling it work. Sounds awesome, right? Well it is. And that's why the competition to become a game tester is harder than beating Contra without the cheat. If you think you have what it takes, check out the job board on GamesTester.com.

☠ $ *tried it* ○

800 **DEVELOP A VIDEO GAME.** Ever thought you could one-up the folks at Microsoft or Nintendo? Go for it. Going from concept to finished product isn't easy (and usually requires an advanced degree), and designing a fully developed game can take years, especially on your own. But remember—if you build it, they will come.

☠ $ $ *tried it* ○

801 **ENTER A VIDEO GAME TOURNAMENT.** Think you have what it takes to go pro? Then put up or shut up and hit up MLGPro.com. (Yes, MLG does stand for Major League Gaming.) This isn't *The Wizard*, so a mastery of Super Mario Bros. 3 won't get you anywhere. These guys (and girls) take their gaming seriously. You might want to try a local tournament first.

☠ $ $ *tried it* ○

802 **BUILD WEBSITES FOR PEOPLE.** The best way for anyone to get noticed in any field nowadays is to have an online presence. While some people might be a star in their industry, they may not have the slightest idea on how to gain attention through a strong website. That's where you come in. Construct an online platform to launch their career.

☠ $ $ *tried it* ○

803 **LAUNCH A WEBSITE FOR A COMPANY.** It's always a hit to a business's credibility when its website looks like it was built using dial-up and Prodigy. If you have some web development skills, shop them around to local businesses looking to gain an online presence.

☠ $ $ *tried it* ○

804 **MAINTAIN A COMPANY'S BLOG.** There's a big difference between running a personal blog and hosting one for a business that expects everything to be up-to-date. Your fifteen readers aren't going to be upset if you skip a Sunday update, or mess up a link. But if you take on blogging duties for a company that expects perfection, be ready to bust out your best blogging skills on the regular.

☠ ☠ $ $ *tried it* ○

805 **START A BLOG—WITH ADS.** Anyone and his mother can register at WordPress.com and begin blogging. However, it takes some exceptional talent to launch a blog, solicit some advertisers, and get enough traffic to his site in order to make money off of it. Get creative. Find and post the next big YouTube sensation, post video-logs that will get repeat visitors, or dish some serious gossip that will make viewers want more. Whatever you do, do it well enough to generate capital.

☠ $ *tried it* ○

Wired Up

806 **SET UP SOMEONE'S COMPUTER.** You might think it's a piece of cake to break a new computer out of its boxes, plug in the necessary wires, and get it up and running without an issue. But that's not the case for everyone. One too many ports or a few too many prompts and the uninitiated will quickly give up on becoming wired. That's where *you* come in.

☠ $ *tried it* ○

807 **CLEAN UP COMPUTERS.** This entry isn't about dusting towers and monitors. It's about getting down to the source of any issues users are having with their PCs. Most problems are caused by a clogging amount of adware, spyware, and viruses that unsuspecting surfers have picked up. If you hear someone complain about how slow her computer's moving, offer to lend a hand.

☠ $ $ *tried it* ○

808 **REPAIR TELEVISIONS.** Now that people are paying thousands of dollars for their LCD flat screens, they're more likely to hire out for a repair when the set goes on the fritz than scrap the one they have and buy a new TV. Just be sure you know what you're doing—otherwise a simple repair could end up in a trip to Best Buy with you footing the bill.

☠ ☠ ☠ $ $ *tried it* ○

809 **HOOK UP SURROUND SOUND.** Plenty of homes have surround-sound ready television sets. However, people don't have the sound engineering know-how to put their TVs' audio abilities to best use. Take care of setting them up and have them take care of padding your wallet. Be careful though—a couple crossed wires and a blown speaker means your wallet will be singing the blues.

☠ ☠ $ $ *tried it* ○

810 **TRANSFER A RECORD COLLECTION TO DIGITAL MUSIC.**
From your eight-year-old nephew to your eighty-year-old
great aunt, young and old alike are rocking out with ear-
buds nowadays. While your nephew doesn't remember a
time where the latest tunes weren't digital, Great Aunt
Mill's favorite jams are trapped in vinyl. Help her put her
music library on her MacBook, and a few bucks in your
pocket.

☠   *$*   *tried it* ○

811 **TURN FILMS INTO DVDS.** Everyone has stacks of old home
videos. The only problem is everyone doesn't have VCRs
anymore. Capitalize on society's switch to discs by bringing
other people's memories up to speed with the digital age.

☠   *$*   *tried it* ○

812 **TURN PHOTOGRAPHS INTO DIGITAL PICTURES.** Even
Grandpa's got a Facebook page, and now he's looking to
post some pics for his grandkids. However, that crazy party
he hosted back in '76 was only documented in Kodak five-
by-sevens. (Someone forgot their digital camera.) Therefore
he needs to transfer all those dusty albums onto a sleek CD.

☠   *$*   *tried it* ○

813 **TOUCH UP DIGITAL PICTURES.** Maybe Gramps has a serious case of red eye (be it from too much flash—or too much
gin). For an additional fee, you can go in and reduce red
eye, brighten up the faded colors, and crop it correctly.
Whether you tack these expenses on to the digitization, or
take on a job where the photos are already digital, you better be sure you know what you're doing so you don't screw
up people's precious moments.

☠ ☠   *$*   *tried it* ○

Wired Up

814 **SELL YOUR PHOTOSHOP SKILLS.** If only your services were available for George in that *Seinfeld* episode where he tried to erase himself from his boss's picture (only to have his boss's face wiped from his family's beach photo). Post your PhotoShop prowess on the services section of craigslist and see if anyone has a Costanza-style situation from which they need to be cut and pasted.

☠ ☠ $ $ *tried it* ○

815 **CREATE A POWERPOINT PRESENTATION.** Sure PowerPoint's a skill that everyone who ever had to take a Microsoft Office tutorial has come to grasp. But if your mastery of the program outshines other slide showers, put it up for sale. Who knows, a PowerPoint by you might be the difference between a promotion and a conference room snoozefest.

☠ $ $ *tried it* ○

816 **REFORMAT A HARD DRIVE.** There are a few firsts in everyone's life that they remember—their first kiss, their first love, and their first time seeing the dreaded "blue screen." While they probably got bit and their heart broken, help them make the best of the blue screen by saving the day and reformatting their hard drive.

☠ $ $ *tried it* ○

817 **TRANSFER FILES FROM AN OLD COMPUTER TO A NEW ONE.** Whether you're rescuing files from a dead CPU, or simply copying over important files from a functional, older model, you can play up how hard the transfer is in order to charge a higher fee. If someone's asking you to complete this task for them, they'll have no idea how hard it really is.

☠ $ $ *tried it* ○

818 **LAUNCH YOUR OWN SEARCH ENGINE.** Google had to start somewhere. What's to say your new take on trolling the Net isn't going to take off? Try working on something that combines the strength of Google with the quirky appeal of first-generation engine AskJeeves.com.

☠   *$ $ $*   *tried it* ○

819 **DEVELOP MYSPACE SKINS.** *OMG! Ur MySpace is sooo gr8!! Lolz!!!* Who has more expendable income than teenage girls? Cash in on these cash cows by giving them what they want—glittery, sparkling, super-cute MySpace skins. Your only risk here is losing any credibility you may have. Enjoy!

☠   *$ $*   *tried it* ○

820 **CRAFT BLOG TEMPLATES.** Sure, people like to read blogs because the writing's interesting and the concept is cool, but most will skip right over any that look like they were put together by a twelve-year-old. That said—a good blog template doesn't have to be busy and buzzing with tons going on. A simple, clean, and functional blog skin can make you some money.

☠   *$ $*   *tried it* ○

821 **CLEAN UP WEBSITES.** Notice a bug on a company's site? Know how to fix it? See if they're willing to supplement your income by buying your online knowledge. Beware: If you screw up the site even more, you'll be liable to pay for a *real* professional to pick up where you left off.

☠ ☠   *$ $*   *tried it* ○

Wired Up

822 **FASHION SECOND LIFE AVATARS.** Those tiny tweaks you have to give an avatar for it to become your virtual doppelganger are enough to drive anyone nuts (not to mention the carpal tunnel you'll soon be suffering). If you have an artistic mouse hand though, you could lend some help to those with a lead clicker finger. Have them send you a photo of what they'd like to look like and then drop some cash in your PayPal account—or transfer over some Linden dollars if that's what you're into.

☠   **$**   *tried it* ○

823 **OPEN A SECOND LIFE NIGHT CLUB.** You'll need to shell out some real-life dough to put up the virtual velvet rope, but as long as your club is poppin' you should make your investment back in cover charges. Look into booking some entertainment and see if any former reality TV stars would be willing to a host a night at your club.

☠ ☠   **$ $**   *tried it* ○

824 **START A SECOND LIFE STRIP CLUB.** Avatars need love too. All you need to do is to hire some lovely ladies to shake it on your virtual stage, put "Pour Some Sugar on Me" in heavy rotation, and set your rate for the Champagne Room. Before you know it, your e-Bada Bing will be where all the guys want to go to watch the ballet.

☠ ☠ ☠   **$ $ $**   *tried it* ○

825 **SELL USER-CREATED VIDEO GAME LEVELS.** As more gaming systems allow for user-generated content, the opportunities to cash in on your creativity grow. Think you have a level that can stump even the most nimble gamer? Put it up for purchase on sites that host such sales. Just be sure what you've developed is actually challenging. No one can bitch louder than a gamer scorned.

☠ ☠   **$**   *tried it* ○

826   **INSTALL A NEW OPERATING SYSTEM.** Every few years Windows and Macintosh come out with an updated OS. Most people ditch their whole computer in favor of updating their current one with the new system. You can help save those people a few bucks, while making some for yourself. Offer your services and update their existing towers and cubes with the company's latest creation.

☠   **$ $**   *tried it* ○

827   **INSTALL RAM.** Eventually computers are outpaced by the software available and need a boost to keep up with what's out there. If you know someone who's complaining about a slow machine, offer to ramp it up by powering their PC with some additional RAM. Be careful, a little too much static and you might wipe the computer clean.

☠ ☠   **$**   *tried it* ○

828   **SLOT-IN AUDIO AND VIDEO CARDS.** As new programs are invented that rely on new technologies, users with older computers will be left in the dark unless they update their A/V hardware. However, most computer owners are wary about cracking open their towers. That's where you come in. Offer your installation skills, but be sure you know what you're doing—otherwise you might end up owing someone a new system.

☠ ☠   **$**   *tried it* ○

829   **AUTOMATE MANUAL WORK FOR OTHERS.** Some people don't know the ins and outs of Excel like you. Instead, they spend their hours toiling away, adding columns, and copying and pasting, when they could be slacking off. Whether you are extremely efficient at Excel, or excel at another program that has hidden tricks which could benefit the cube drones—you can cash in on those talents. Post them on craigslist and wait to see what happens.

☠   **$**   *tried it* ○

Wired Up

830 **SET UP SOMEONE'S WIRELESS NETWORK.** If you've ever felt the frustration of watching your wireless modem report that there are no available networks even though you spent twenty minutes plugging in a router and installing software—this entry is not for you. However, if you've ever had to fix this problem, you can score big. Take advantage of others' ignorance to the magical world of wireless.

☠ $ $ *tried it* ○

831 **SET UP A WEBCAM FOR SOMEONE.** As people start staying in touch using services like Skype, more and more computer users are turning to webcams to see each other across cyberspace. However, Grandma might have a little more trouble hooking up her newly purchased hardware than her grandkids.

☠ $ *tried it* ○

832 **SELL CLIPART.** Believe it or not, some people still use clipart. Whether it's for school projects, fliers, or menus, those little illustrations remain in demand. You can make some quick cash by generating these files by request.

☠ $ *tried it* ○

833 **BE AN ON-CALL TECH SUPPORT PROFESSIONAL.** You have to know one or two people who have the innate ability to break whatever piece of technology they touch. Don't curse them. Charge them. Give them your cell phone number and let them call whenever they run into trouble. Remember though—you're charging to be on-call whenever, so you run the risk of having to drop whatever you're doing.

☠ ☠ $ $ *tried it* ○

834 **START A NEW MESSAGE BOARD.** If you think message boards are a thing of the past, think again. They're still widely used by gamers and techies to keep tabs on what's hip. Some of the latest web sensations have gained popularity on message boards (see: *I Can Has Cheezburger?*). Don't think companies haven't taken notice. A popular board reaches a lucrative audience and can mean cash for the owner—with the risk of losing your cred.

☠ ☠   *$ $ $*   *tried it* ○

835 **BECOME A BETA USER.** Keep your ear to the blogosphere. Next time you hear about companies getting ready to launch a new site or service, contact them. Chances are they're hiring beta users to bang on it and see if there are any issues.

☠   *$*   *tried it* ○

836 **INSTALL HARDWARE.** Often when people purchase new hardware for their computers, they don't research the compatibility close enough. Therefore, many find that they can't get the piece of equipment they just splurged on to function. That's where you come in. Solve their compatibility issues and make a little commission in the process.

☠   *$ $*   *tried it* ○

837 **UNINSTALL HARDWARE.** Sometimes users force incompatible equipment onto their computers, which ends up causing a downward spiral for their PC. If that's the case, someone (*you*) can make some money going in and fixing what they did wrong. Just don't make matters worse.

☠ ☠   *$ $*   *tried it* ○

838 **MOD GAMING CONSOLES.** The reason you know how to mod a console is because you're developing your own game. Not because you want to play games you've illegally downloaded online and burnt. (Nod.) The reason you would charge others for you to mod their consoles is so they too can try to develop their own video games. (Nod, again.)

☠ ☠ ☠ $ $ *tried it* ○

839 **PROTECT OTHERS AGAINST ONLINE IDENTITY THEFT.** Everyone's worried about getting their identity stolen nowadays. With online banking and shopping, there is a definite need to worry. However, with the proper protection, everyone should be comfortable doing whatever they want online. If you know how to secure yourself on the Internet, provide that service to others so they can come out of the shadows.

☠ $ $ *tried it* ○

840 **HIRE OUT YOUR GRAPHIC DESIGN SKILLS.** So you say you're a pro at InDesign. Show the world what you have to offer by setting an hourly rate and going on the hunt for freelance work. Check out the job sites and craigslist board, but be sure your resume is designed to impress. No one wants to hire a designer with an ugly resume.

☠ $ $ *tried it* ○

841 **BECOME A WEB MASTER.** Maybe you're not the master of *your* domain, but you could be in charge of someone else's. Like with anything, day-to-day issues arise for site owners. If these people are too busy to care, pick up their slack.

☠ ☠ $ $ $ *tried it* ○

842 **HTML CODE FOR CASH.** Just because someone has a solid concept for a site doesn't mean they have the know-how to really step it up online. That's where you come in. Take their concept to the next level with your creative coding. Be prepared for some backlash, though, if their site doesn't take off.

☠ ☠   *$ $*   ***tried it*** ○

843 **DO SOME FREELANCE FLASH WORK.** If someone wants to go one above with site design, one choice is to have some fancy Flash open up upon entering their domain. Get together a sample of what you can do and get proactive. Contact site owners who could use some Flash-work and deliver a concept that will knock their site out of the park.

☠   *$ $*   ***tried it*** ○

844 **C++ PROGRAM FOR PAY.** *Ah, C++* . . . the language of love—for computer geeks. A mastery of this software programming skill can net you some major dough. Still used for writing software, you can pick up a sweet freelancing gig if you're fluent.

☠   *$ $*   ***tried it*** ○

845 **DEVELOP AN IPHONE GAME.** If you know what terms like "Interface Builder" and "UITableView" mean, then you can probably figure out how to develop an iPhone game. It seems like every jackass who is willing to spend 300 bucks on a phone has one of these, and while some people supposedly use their iPhones for business, a lot of people just really love Tetris. Why not develop the next best thing? Put on your nerd glasses and go to work.

☠   *$ $ $*   ***tried it*** ○

Wired Up

CHAPTER 14

Get Schooled

The saying goes, "Those who do *do*, and those who don't, *teach*." However, those people obviously don't know how much money you *do* make by *teaching*. Here are some ideas on how to put your instructing skills to use.

846 **SUBSTITUTE TEACH.** School systems *always* need substitute teachers. Regular teachers call in sick all the time. If you can keep order in a classroom (which means getting their attention, stopping fights, and judiciously using the threat of the vice principal's wrath) you can pick up a daily fee.

☠ $ $ $ *tried it* ○

847 **TUTOR.** This is really cool. You're only dealing with one kid at a time, so you may actually get some teaching done. Of course, you've got to know something about the subject you're teaching, but you've got a college degree, right? You remember something about math? Or history? Or English?

☠ $ $ *tried it* ○

848 **TEACH ENGLISH TO NONNATIVE SPEAKERS.** Thousands of immigrants or foreign visitors want to speak and write English more perfectly. Who better to teach them than you? You can make contacts through your local college or community college and set up individual contracts.

☠ $ $ *tried it* ○

849 **TEACH A FOREIGN LANGUAGE TO A NATIVE SPEAKER.** The globe gets smaller every year, and anyone who wants to get ahead needs a foreign language. This is where you come in. Get out your French dictionary from high school, polish up your Spanish verbs, and review your Russian vocabulary. Advertise online and in local papers for pupils.

☠ $ $ *tried it* ○

850 **SELL TERM PAPERS.** We're getting close to the edge here. But students need term papers, and you can supply them. Be careful how you advertise this, since there are a lot of rules against it. But if you play it right, you can spend a couple of hours researching and writing and pick up a nice fee.

☠ ☠ ☠ $ $ *tried it* ○

851 **START A CRAM STUDY SERVICE.** Everyone knows the best studying is done at the last minute. And everyone knows that you need someone to help you cram. Put an ad on the Internet, featuring your special subject knowledge, and make some money from a student desperate to pass that final exam.

☠ $ *tried it* ○

852 **COACH A SCHOOL'S SPORTS TEAM.** Americans are sports crazy. Where else in the world would 25,000 people turn out for a high school football team. Now you can put yourself in the center of the action as coach of football, basketball, baseball, lacrosse . . . well, you get the idea.

☠ $ $ $ *tried it* ○

853 **CORRECT STANDARDIZED TESTS.** President Bush signed the No Child Left Behind Act, and suddenly standardized tests were at the center of the educational process. While most of these tests are computer graded, some still need a human touch. Get in touch with your local board of education to find out about opportunities for grading.

☠ $ $ *tried it* ○

Get Schooled

854 **COME UP WITH QUESTIONS FOR STANDARDIZED TESTS.**
Like we said, the name of the game today is tests, tests,
tests. And someone's got to make them up. Schools and
school boards are desperate for questions to put on the
exams. Check in with your local school authorities.

☠ $ *tried it* ○

855 **PROCTOR A STANDARDIZED TEST.** How else can you earn
money while sitting on your ass? Now that the economy
is so bad, many people are heading off to college and grad
school where they can sit it out while the country rebounds.
This means more people are taking the SATs, ACTs, and
GREs, which puts proctors in high demand. Good news for
you . . . and your wallet!

☠ $ $ *tried it* ○

856 **CREATE WORKSHEETS FOR TEACHERS.** Teachers are
about the most overworked professionals in the country.
They're always in need of help. Use your knowledge to put
together worksheets for their classes. They'll be eternally
grateful, and they'll pay you for it.

☠ $ *tried it* ○

857 **SELL LESSON PLANS.** What harassed high school teacher
wouldn't pay a few bucks for a premade lesson plan? They
might even pay you to recommend readings or create
hyperlinks they can pass on to their students. The teaching
profession needs help, and you can be on the spot to give it.

☠ $ *tried it* ○

858 **TUTOR FOR THE SAT/ACT.** These days more and more people see college as the solution to their problems. But before they get into college, they've got to pass certain tests. Remember back to when you took the SAT or the ACT and make money by telling others what got you past them.

☠ $ $ *tried it* ○

859 **TUTOR FOR THE GMAT.** If you've got an MBA, you know you've got to pass the GMAT (Graduate Management Admission Test) to get into business school. And there are more and more MBAs these days. So dust off your old test papers and tell prospective business majors you're their best hope for success.

☠ $ $ *tried it* ○

860 **TUTOR FOR THE LSAT.** "First thing, let's kill all the lawyers." Well, Shakespeare may have said that, but these days there are more lawyers than ever. And aspiring lawyers have to pass the Law School Admission Test. You're their last, best hope. And you can charge for it.

☠ $ $ *tried it* ○

861 **TUTOR FOR THE GED.** Lots of people drop out of high school. And lots of people want to get their General Education Degree later on so they can move up the ladder in their company. But they've got to pass the GED standardized test. If you remember your high school classes, you can tutor GED students.

☠ $ *tried it* ○

862 **SELL BOOK SUMMARIES.** Too many business execs today are super-busy with no time to read the latest bestsellers in their field. You can write a 100- to 200-word summary and sell it to them. You'll be making them look smart, and they'll be making you richer.

☠ $ *tried it* ○

863 **BECOME A PRIVATE TUTOR TO PRESCHOOLERS.** More and more parents want their kids to get into *the* schools. But that means getting tutors in preschools to prepare them. This is your chance to benefit from the snobbishness of America's top class.

☠ $ $ *tried it* ○

864 **TEACH AT AN AFTER-SCHOOL PROGRAM.** Sometimes they're for gifted teens. Sometimes they're for adults who want to get ahead. Either way, there's room for you to benefit from your knowledge and experience by teaching. Contact the local board of education for opportunities.

☠ $ $ *tried it* ○

865 **RUN A HIGH SCHOOL EXTRACURRICULAR ACTIVITY.** From the archaeological society to the Latin club, there's tons of stuff after school that needs a strong, helping hand. And schools are happy to pay those hands. Some phone calls to your nearby high schools can really pay off.

☠ $ *tried it* ○

866 **RUN A CREATIVE WRITING PROGRAM.** Do you think you've got the next William Faulkner living next door? Maybe your neighbor is harboring a secret Jackie Collins novel that she's just not sure about. Offer your expertise in critiquing their work and find an undiscovered genius.

☠ $ $ *tried it* ○

Get Schooled

867 **TEACH MUSIC LESSONS.** Did you play French horn in high school? What about clarinet? Or electric guitar? In any case, that music education can come in handy. In your neighborhood, there's a kid who wants to be the next Eric Clapton. Why not give him a head start—for a small fee?

☠   *$ $*   *tried it* ○

868 **GIVE SINGING LESSONS.** *Do, re, mi, fa, so, la, ti, doooo!* If you know how to work the pipes to make beautiful music, hire out your vocal coaching skills. It doesn't matter whether your students want to sing arias or on *American Idol*—as long as their checks clear, you're good to go.

☠   *$ $*   *tried it* ○

869 **TEACH COMPUTER SKILLS.** Maybe Photoshop and Excel come naturally to you? Maybe you think Basic and Java are simple. If that's the case, your local community college can probably use your skills teaching evening computing classes for adults. Give them a call.

☠   *$ $*   *tried it* ○

870 **BECOME A YOGI.** Do you know how to bend your legs behind your head? Well, it's not so simple for the rest of us. Roll up your mat and yoga ball and head on over to the community college's Center for Continuing Education. They're always glad of a little expertise.

☠   *$ $*   *tried it* ○

871 **TEACH MOM-AND-ME YOGA.** Nothing says mother-daughter bonding like sweating together in a yoga class. And nothing pays like teaching moms and girls to come together on a yoga mat. Your local community center may offer some great opportunities to teach classes for older and younger women.

☠   *$*   *tried it* ○

Get Schooled

872 **TEACH MARTIAL ARTS.** Tae kwon do. Judo. Karate. You can't turn around these days without seeing a martial arts academy. Offer your skills in teaching, and you may just be able to punch your way to big bucks. Check your local paper for ads.

☠️ $ $ *tried it* ○

873 **BE A TOUR GUIDE AT A LOCAL PLACE OF INTEREST.** Love history? Why not make some money off that passion. There are tourist locales in every city in the United States, and all of them need someone thoroughly educated in the role that they've played in history. To find a tourist trap near you, check out *www.fodors.com*.

☠️ $ $ *tried it* ○

874 **READY A FOREIGNER FOR THE CITIZENSHIP EXAM.** Hate to break it to you, but the questions on the U.S. citizenship exam are harder than you'd think. Testees have to answer questions like "How many stripes are there on the U.S. flag?" "What INS form is used to apply to become a naturalized citizen?" and "What are the first ten amendments to the Constitution called?" You'll not only be earning some Benjamins, but educating yourself about American history as well.

☠️ $ $ *tried it* ○

875 **GIVE DRIVING LESSONS.** This may be scary, but really how bad can it be? Most kids today have spent so much time pretending to drive on their PS2s and Wiis that teaching them how to drive in the real world should be a breeze. Even so, it's probably a good idea to start them out in a deserted parking lot.

☠️ ☠️ ☠️ $ $ *tried it* ○

876 **TEACH A CLASS AT A RETIREMENT HOME.** You may not be able to teach an old dog new tricks, but you can teach seniors. Seniors need to keep their minds and bodies active, so anything from English literature to quilting is up for grabs. Find a retirement home near you at *www.retirement homes.com.*

☠ $ $ *tried it* ○

877 **SHOW PEOPLE HOW TO KNIT.** It seems like everyone's knitting nowadays, so pick up those needles and teach someone how to knit one, pearl two. After all, the people you teach will be helping the local economy when those potholders, sweaters, and scarves are sold at local craft fairs. For all things knitting, check out *http://knitting.about.com.*

☠ $ $ *tried it* ○

878 **RUN A HOME-ECONOMICS COURSE.** With the rigorous restructuring of school systems' curriculum based on standardized testing, subjects like home economics have been cut in favor of an emphasis on math and reading. While this restructuring may help with test scores, it leaves students in the dark about real-world skills. Offer your cooking, cleaning, and sewing skills to students who want to know how to run an organized home.

☠ $ $ *tried it* ○

879 **TEACH WOODWORKING.** Many home improvement stores run monthly classes on how to build handmade wooden goods. Take a page out of their books and turn your garage into your very own hammer and nail classroom. The corporate big-shots can do it—why can't you? Just be sure you can handle talking and demonstrating at the same time. Otherwise you might come out of the class a few digits lighter.

☠ ☠ ☠ $ $ *tried it* ○

880 **TEACH OTHERS HOW TO TEACH.** Want to teach, but have no idea what? Teaching others how to teach solves that problem. How to create a syllabus. How to control a classroom. How to put together a lesson plan. You're good to go. You may even be able to save yourself time by having your students grade each other's work. Be careful, though. If you don't have confidence in your teaching ability, your students will eat you alive.

☠ ☠　　　$ $ $ $　　*tried it* ○

881 **BECOME AN AP TUTOR.** More and more students are trying to save money on college by receiving college credits their senior year of high school. Help them out and take some of that "saved" money for yourself. Shouldn't be too hard. You've probably taken most of these classes already anyway.

☠　　　$ $　　*tried it* ○

882 **READY A STUDENT FOR COLLEGE.** Do you remember being a freshman? Scared, unsure what to expect, low man on the totem pole. Make sure the student you take under your wing doesn't go through the same things you did. Instead, for a fee, teach them all they need to know to make it through their first semester. With advice ranging from not signing up for an 8 A.M. class to how to get into a senior party, you'll be a priceless asset to your little freshman.

☠　　　$ $　　*tried it* ○

883 **BE A CAMP COUNSELOR.** Remember camp classics like *Bug Juice*, *Salute Your Shorts*, and *The Parent Trap*? You can enjoy all the fun of summer camp, make some bank . . . and be the one in charge! Sounds like a great way to spend the summer. Find your counseling job at *www.camp channel.com/jobboard.*

☠　　　$ $ $　　*tried it* ○

884 **TEACH SUMMER SCHOOL.** Come on. You know what summer school is all about: hot, stuffy classrooms, disgruntled students, and lazy lesson plans. Why not take this knowledge and use it to get yourself a summer job. You'll be able to sympathize with your students as far as being stuck inside on a humid summer's day is concerned, and they'll love you for it.

☠   *$ $ $*   *tried it* ○

885 **TEACH GYMNASTICS.** You don't even have to be flexible. Remember, those who can, do; those who can't, teach. Anyway, you'll probably be teaching kids who won't realize that you didn't train under Bella Karolyi. As long as you can do a somersault, you're good to go—to the bank! For more info about U.S. gymnastics, check out *www.usa-gymnastics.org.*

☠ ☠   *$ $ $*   *tried it* ○

886 **BECOME AN ACTING COACH.** What does it take to teach acting? Basically you spend a few hours a few days a week listening to people complain about their lives and then watching them pretend to be someone else. You do some of this in your own life anyway, so you may as well get paid for it.

☠   *$ $*   *tried it* ○

887 **TEACH A SWIMMING CLASS.** Are you patient? Supportive? Know how to do the breaststroke and hold your breath under water? You don't even have to venture into the deep end to teach a beginner the basics of swimming. All you have to do is keep them afloat to ensure your bank account stays the same.

☠ ☠   *$ $*   *tried it* ○

888 **BECOME A PERSONAL COACH.** Let's face it. We all have someone in our lives who can't get his or her act together and is a total slacker. Offer up your services and help them get their life back on track—for a price of course. Acting as a friend's personal coach may be the best-case scenario. You already have to listen to her bitch about her job or significant other. Now, you can tell her exactly what you think—and charge her for your honesty. Sounds like a good idea to me!

☠ ☠ $ $ *tried it* ○

889 **TEACH AN ADULT LEARNING CLASS.** Who likes working with kids anyway? Adults are a lot easier to teach because they want to be there, can afford to pay you, and have less time to do homework, which means less grading for you. Don't worry if you've never taught before. As long as you stay one chapter ahead of your students, you're good to go.

☠ ☠ $ $ $ *tried it* ○

890 **WORK AS AN AU PAIR.** Like kids? Working as a nanny may be the perfect job for you. What other 9-to-5 job pays for your food and housing, pays you a salary, and gives you the opportunity to take "business trips" where you get to do more than sit in a boardroom? Go to *www.aupair.com* or *www.greataupair.com* to learn more.

☠ $ $ $ *tried it* ○

891 **HELP STUDENTS APPLY FOR SCHOLARSHIPS.** With the high cost of a college education today, every prospective college student is looking for a handout—in the guise of a scholarship. The only problem with this free money scheme is that it takes hours and hours of filling out paperwork and writing essay after essay to prove that they're worthy. Why not take some of the pressure off of these future scholars and make a few bucks for yourself at the same time by doing their paperwork for them. After all, how hard can it be?

☠ $ *tried it* ○

Get Schooled

892 **TRANSLATE DOCUMENTS.** This job not only pads your wallet, but sounds good when you're talking to strangers, "Yes, I'm a *translator*." Don't speak a foreign language? Not a problem. Just use translation software. You can also do this for free at *http://babelfish.yahoo.com*.

☠ ☠ ☠ $ $ $ *tried it* ○

893 **GIVE ART LESSONS.** Picture yourself a Picasso or a Monet? Well, teach what you know and paint the town red. You don't even really have to have any artistic talent. Impressionism anyone? So gather up your Cray-Pas and get going!

☠ $ $ *tried it* ○

894 **DEVELOP COLLEGE ESSAYS.** Good at English? Help your ESL roommate be good at English too by correcting his crappy essay. Here's the premise: Your roommate/friend/person who answers your ad on craigslist.com writes a lousy essay for their American lit class. They pass it off to you and you correct their grammar, spelling, and citations. Voila! A+ essay for them. An easy $50 in cash for you!

☠ ☠ $ *tried it* ○

895 **WRITE COLLEGE ESSAYS.** Who doesn't miss the days of fifteen-page papers and late-night caffeine binges? Right. . . . Anyway, as a college-essay writing expert, you can help save others from the fate you were subjected to. The good news? Oftentimes, students looking to buy essays aren't looking for A-level work. After all, how can someone who's barely managed a D average expect to fool their teacher by using words like "deconstructionism" and "discourse." Be careful, though . . . this isn't exactly an ethical way to earn a living.

☠ ☠ $ $ $ *tried it* ○

896 **BECOME A SKI INSTRUCTOR.** Do you look forward to hitting the slopes all summer long? Can't wait to be outside, skiing on untouched snow, breathing in the crisp mountain air? Well, you may as well put your passion to work making cold hard cash. After all, if you're going down the mountain anyway, why not take someone along with you? You can get your ski time in and get a good laugh when your student falls on his ass.

☠ $ $ *tried it* ○

897 **TEACH SNOWBOARDING.** Snowboarding is the next frontier of winter athletic competition. It made its Olympic debut in the 2006 Torino Games, proving it has staying power. You need to be a certified instructor, so check out the American Association of Snowboard Instructors (*www.aasi.org*).

☠ ☠ $ $ *tried it* ○

898 **GIVE HORSEBACK-RIDING LESSONS.** Don't have a horse? No worries. Get a job at a stable instead. All you have to do is manage to stay on and enjoy the ride—and make sure your student does the same. Sometimes horseback riding can be a painful experience, but it will be a lot easier to deal with if your butt is padded with cash.

☠ ☠ $ $ *tried it* ○

899 **DO SCHOLARLY RESEARCH.** Love the library? Anyone in academia spends enough time there and would love to pay you to go for them. Best of all, you won't be the one pulling an all-nighter to finish that paper. To find a job as a research assistant, check online job sites like *www.monster.com* or *www.hotjobs.com*, academic search sites like *www.higheredjobs.com*, or the websites of your local college or university.

☠ $ $ *tried it* ○

900 **OUTLINE PAPERS.** Devising an outline is the hardest part of writing a paper; once you've got it, the paper all but writes itself. Even good students have trouble, so there's a huge market for your services. Advertise on craigslist in college towns.

☠ $ *tried it* ○

901 **TEACH MAGIC TRICKS.** Show a class how to pull a quarter out of a volunteer's ear and watch your bank account fill up like, well, magic. Just make sure you know your tricks or you might have to stage your own disappearing act.

☠ ☠ $ $ *tried it* ○

902 **SELL YOUR NOTES ONLINE.** You're the only person in the history of college to attend every single 9 A.M. comparative politics lecture. Take full advantage of your awesomeness and post an ad on craigslist offering to sell your complete notes.

☠ $ *tried it* ○

903 **TEACH ICE SKATING.** Cash in on your ability to execute a camel (the spin, not the mammal). But consider yourself warned: any sport that combines ice, sharp blades, and Tonya Harding is not for the faint of heart. Check out the Professional Skaters Association (*www.skatepsa.com*).

☠ ☠ $ *tried it* ○

904 BE A PREGNANCY COACH. Pregnancy can be scary and overwhelming, so your job is to answer questions, soothe fears, and teach expectant moms about proper nutrition, exercise, and stress management so they can welcome a perfectly healthy and happy bundle of joy.

☠ $ $ *tried it* ○

905 HOST A LAMAZE CLASS. You don't necessarily have to be a Lamaze-certified instructor, but it helps you network and it gives you credibility with jittery first-time parents. Visit Lamaze International (*www.lamaze.org*) to find more information about membership and classes.

☠ $ $ *tried it* ○

906 TEACH DANCING. Whether you teach former frat boys to waltz for their impending wedding days or organize a ballet class for six-year-olds in tutus, dancing lessons can be surprisingly lucrative. But did we mention your toes bleed when you learn to dance *en pointe*?

☠ ☠ $ *tried it* ○

907 BECOME AN ACADEMIC SUPERVISOR. You're like a tutor who doesn't have to know calculus. Parents will hire you to keep their high school or college student in line. Devise study plans, track grades, and don't be afraid to crack the whip to get results.

☠ $ $ *tried it* ○

908 TEACH SOMEONE HOW TO READ. If you can specialize in learning disabilities, do it. It's a great hook if you can produce results. Post your resume on craigslist and look for posts asking for reading tutors in your area.

☠ $ $ *tried it* ○

909 **TEACH AN ARTS AND CRAFTS COURSE.** Share the joy of your favorite hobby by teaching courses. Partner with your local paint store or camera shop and introduce beginners to your craft. Also check adult education centers, but be aware that they may require more extensive credentials.

☠ $ *tried it* ○

910 **CREATE STUDY GUIDES.** Do you know what the green light in *The Great Gatsby* symbolizes? There are thousands of students who don't have the time or the patience (or maybe the brains) to figure it out for themselves and will gladly pay you for your wisdom. Make a website and start selling.

☠ $ *tried it* ○

911 **TEACH STAND-UP.** If your repertoire is limited to knock-knock jokes, sit back down. But if you've got what it takes to nurture the next Letterman, step right up. Check with local comedy clubs and continuing education centers—or start your own comedy academy.

☠ $ $ *tried it* ○

912 **TRANSCRIBE LECTURES.** This can be a very valuable service for students who have learning disabilities or who are unable to make a class. Some professors will let you put a tape recorder next to the lectern, but others object to recordings.

☠ ☠ $ *tried it* ○

913 **GIVE SURFING INSTRUCTIONS.** Spend your days teaching tourists to hang ten. It's like getting paid to go on vacation. We feel it is incumbent upon us to mention the one minor drawback: sharks with razor-sharp teeth. Check out the National Surf Schools & Instructors Association (*www.nssia.org*).

☠ ☠ ☠ $ $ *tried it* ○

914 **GIVE LESSONS IN SPEAKING "AMERICAN."** Pack your bags and grab your passport because you're Bangalore-bound. Companies in Asia place a huge emphasis on speaking "American" English, so you can actually get paid for teaching people to imitate your nasally Midwestern accent.

☠ ☠ $ *tried it* ○

915 **TEACH UNSKILLED LABORERS.** There will always be a demand for unskilled labor, but you can help train people so they can further their careers. And you never know—the experience might come in handy in your own career.

☠ $ *tried it* ○

916 **EDIT SCHOLARLY PAPERS.** Academics are often very smart people—but just because they've discovered that the deterioration of the thingamawhatsit is directly related to the onset of meningoencephawhatever doesn't mean they can write a coherent sentence about it. You'll have to be a lot better at the scholarly jargon than we are, though.

☠ $ $ *tried it* ○

917 **BE A CREDIT COUNSELOR.** People who have financially overextended themselves often find themselves in the unpleasant position of paying someone to tell them the best way to pay down their debt. You may want to ask for payment up front. In cash.

☠ ☠ $ $ *tried it* ○

918 **GIVE POTTERY LESSONS.** Archaeologists can tell a lot from the pottery shards they unearth when they excavate ancient civilizations. What future generations will make of the clay dinosaurs you teach summer camp kids to make is anyone's guess.

☠ $ *tried it* ○

919 **TEACH ETIQUETTE.** Gentle Reader: Miss Manners encourages you to share the guidelines of proper decorum with the other members of your generation. Student organizations such as fraternities and sororities and service sector employers are the most likely to take advantage of your services.

☠ $ $ *tried it* ○

920 **CRITIQUE ESSAYS.** How much is it worth to earn an A in English? You can find out by charging a consultation fee to edit students' essays. Best of all, making your services available online lets you reach paying customers anywhere in the world.

☠ $ $ *tried it* ○

921 **CERTIFY OTHERS IN SCUBA.** Help others gain the skills they need to explore shipwrecks and coral reefs. First things first, you need to be a strong swimmer and you must be certified in scuba. PADI (*www.padi.com*) is a good place to start.

☠ ☠ $ $ *tried it* ○

922 **TAKE NOTES FOR COLLEGE STUDENTS.** The brothers of Delta Tau Chi can nurse the hangovers they got from your Beirut tournament (entry 29) while you take notes at their lectures. If you're not a student, make sure you can get into the lecture halls without a university-issued ID.

☠ $ *tried it* ○

Get Schooled

251

923 **CERTIFY OTHERS IN CPR.** Medical professionals are required to keep their certification up to date, so there's never a shortage of people to take these classes. Check out the American Heart Association's certification courses (*www.americanheart.org/cpr*).

☠   **$**   *tried it* ○

924 **GIVE POKER LESSONS.** Think you could show those guys on *World Series of Poker* what's up? Why don't you start by teaching individuals with less gambling knowledge how to take it to the river. There's less of a chance that you will get schooled by doing so—though the level of embarrassment if you get trumped by your tutee antes up the risk level.

☠ ☠   **$ $**   *tried it* ○

925 **HOMESCHOOL OTHER PEOPLE'S KIDS.** Just because you can't stand your own children, doesn't mean you can't get down to some good ol' homeschooling. If you're qualified, hire out as an at-home one-on-one teacher for kids with overprotective parents.

☠   **$ $ $**   *tried it* ○

926 **SHARE YOUR NEGOTIATION SKILLS.** It's becoming more and more important to know what you're going to do and what you're going to say before you go into your boss and ask for a raise. Therefore, if someone—like *you*—knows how to handle this type of precarious situation, then capitalize on that set of skills, and teach people how to handle it as well. The higher the raise, the higher your commission—just don't get your student fired.

☠ ☠   **$ $ $**   *tried it* ○

Get Schooled

927 **TEACH OTHERS HOW TO TAKE THE NEXT PROFESSIONAL STEP.** Sometimes people hit a professional plateau. They're good at what they're doing, but they don't know what they need to do to get to the next level. If you've scaled your industry's corporate ladder, make your insight available to people stuck on a middle rung—for a price.

☠ $ $ $ *tried it* ○

928 **GIVE LESSONS IN MAKEUP APPLICATION.** If someone unintentionally looks like a drag queen, chances are she needs some help in applying makeup. Tactfully ask if she wants some guidance in using powder and gloss.

☠ ☠ $ $ *tried it* ○

929 **WORK AS A SPEAKING COACH.** Everyone hated their mandatory course in public speaking. That distaste for public discourse, however, can cause some issues in how one handles himself in front of a group. These are the types of people who need extra help when delivering speeches. Drop some helpful oratory knowledge and refine the way they speak.

☠ $ $ *tried it* ○

930 **SELL YOURSELF AS A SALES GURU.** Can you make anyone buy anything? Than maybe you can help others sharpen the way they hock their wares. Offer one-on-one advice for a price.

☠ $ $ *tried it* ○

Get Schooled

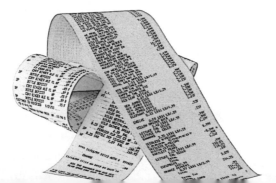

931 **INSTRUCT REALITY-TELEVISION WANNABES.** You would think auditioning for a reality show would be pretty simple, right? Wrong. Apparently there are people who are willing to pay for application education in order to secure their spot on the next show. While you might not be as big-time as The New York Reality TV School (which is getting its own show), you can offer some lessons on how to be "real" enough to make it.

☠ $ $ *tried it* ○

932 **LEAD SUBSTANCE-ABUSE SEMINARS.** Put your nightmarish experiences dealing with addiction to good use. Hire out as a speaker who educates on the horrors of being hooked to drugs or alcohol. Colleges will often include such seminars in their orientation programs. Contact local schools to see if you can set up speaking gigs.

☠ ☠ $ $ $ *tried it* ○

933 **COACH COACHES ABOUT COACHING.** Are you the Lombardi of high school sports? Put your stellar coaching skills to good use then and teach others how to motivate, inspire, and get the same type of results. Coaches probably aren't the most receptive audiences—they are used to leading, after all—but if you can keep their attention and make them better, you're golden.

☠ ☠ $ $ $ *tried it* ○

934 **GIVE SHOOTING LESSONS.** If you're a skilled sharpshooter, hit the range and see if anyone is in need of some kill-shot pointers. Look for those gunners who completely miss the mark and get them to pay for your dead-eye expertise. Just remember who you're dealing with—they might miss their targets, but chances are they'd hit you in a misfire.

☠ ☠ ☠ $ $ *tried it* ○

935 **BECOME AN ONLINE PROFESSOR.** If you're a college professor with some extra time on your hands (say, June, July, and August), consider becoming an online professor. It may involve some work up front, but the time commitment is minimal and you can't beat the commute.

☠   *$ $ $*   *tried it* ○

936 **EDUCATE OTHERS ON SURVIVAL SKILLS.** Whether they're preparing to live in a post-Apocalyptic world, or just hoping to make it on the next season of *Survivor*, there are plenty of people looking to learn how to make it on their own in the wilderness. Show them the ins and outs of building shelter, eating berries and bugs, and starting the all-important fire.

☠   *$ $*   *tried it* ○

CHAPTER 15

Cook Up Some Cash

You might not be Martha or Rocco, but as long as you're skilled in the kitchen—and don't scare away diners—you have an opportunity to make some money off your culinary abilities.

937 **PUT UP A LEMONADE STAND.** It's not just for kids anymore. Choose the right busy corner and offer a variety of lemonade flavors—raspberry, mango, peach. You may even offer juices and other snacks. In fact, it could turn into quite a little street food business if you work it right.

☠ $ **tried it** ○

938 **CATER AN EVENT.** You don't need a big operation to cater, just a normal kitchen with a good working oven and refrigerator. Solicit your first jobs from friends and acquaintances and, if you do well, word will quickly spread. Clip recipes from magazines and invest in an appetizer cookbook.

☠ $ $ **tried it** ○

939 **BARTEND AT A FRIEND'S PARTY.** You do what you have to do, and if that means missing out on being the guest passed out on your friend's floor at the end of the night . . . so be it. This time offer to bartend the party. Be sure to watch *Cocktail* to brush up on your cup-juggling skills.

☠ ☠ $ $ **tried it** ○

940 **BARTEND AT A RESTAURANT.** Okay, you don't need to be Tom Cruise in *Cocktail*. Spending some time in bars (it's a hardship, I know!) and a couple of hours with a bartender's guide to mixed drinks will give you the basic know-how. And if you stick with it long enough, you may learn to juggle cocktail shakers.

☠ $ $ **tried it** ○

941 **MIX A SIGNATURE DRINK.** There's a difference between being a bartender and being a mixologist. Bartenders serve up drinks created by others; mixologists create their own unique concoctions. The tips and crowds will be better if you're able to come up with a specialty drink that gets people talking and sitting at *your* bar for *your* drink.

☠ $ $ $ **tried it** ○

942 **MAKE JAMS AND PRESERVES.** Buy fruit in bulk at your local farmer's market and turn your kitchen into an assembly line, mashing, boiling, and canning. You can enlist family members in this, and reward them with some homemade raspberry jam on their toast the next morning.

☠️ $ *tried it* ○

943 **OPEN YOUR OWN MICROBREWERY.** This will require some significant outlay if you're going to be serious about it. You can set it up in your garage or basement if they're reasonably temperature controlled. Beer-making kits won't really produce the amount you need to make money; look at sales of secondhand equipment for a big brewing vat.

☠️ ☠️ $ $ *tried it* ○

944 **INFUSE YOUR OWN LIQUORS.** You'll need some big jars, a couple of bags of sugar, six or seven gallons of *cheap* vodka (expensive vodka doesn't work as well), and fruit such as raspberries, strawberries, peaches, and apricots. Store the steeping liquor in a dark place like your cellar. And invest in some nice bottles to sell it in.

☠️ $ $ *tried it* ○

945 **BOTTLE YOUR OWN WINE.** Ideally, grow your own grapes, too, but if you can't manage that, buy grapes from the farmer's market. Your kids will be happy to take off their shoes and tramp around in them, mashing them to a nice pulp for the fermenting process. Start saving old wine bottles; you can reuse them for your own vintage.

☠️ ☠️ ☠️ $ $ *tried it* ○

Cook Up Some Cash

946 **BECOME A SOMMELIER.** If people actually listen when you start talking about wine then clearly you know your stuff (or you're a good BSer). Put that knowledge to good use by becoming a sommelier. Many community colleges and adult ed institutions have courses that you can take to bone up on the vino.

☠ $ $ $ *tried it* ○

947 **PLAN MENUS FOR RESTAURANTS.** Are you a foodie with a talent for organization? Congratulations—you're a menu consultant. Create some sample menus, drop them off at restaurants, and offer your talents for a fee. You probably can't charge more than a couple hundred dollars, but the free samples are worth something.

☠ $ $ *tried it* ○

948 **SET UP A TAILGATE STAND.** Who doesn't love a tailgate party? At the next big high school football game, set up your own stand selling chili, hot dogs, hamburgers, and soft drinks. If you make it a regular thing, word will quickly spread. No matter who wins the match, you'll still be ahead of the game.

☠ $ *tried it* ○

949 **SELL YOUR SECRET PASTA SAUCE.** We know, we know. First you have to *have* a secret sauce. Well, remember that vodka sauce you used at the last potluck? The one all your guests loved? Jazz it up a little, print it out on nice, neat cards with some attractive calligraphy, and see just how much people will pay for it.

☠ $ $ *tried it* ○

950 **CREATE YOUR OWN COOKBOOK.** Once you've got a couple of sauces together along with Grandma's recipe for ginger cookies and Great Aunt Beatrice's special meatloaf, start pulling together a cookbook. Experiment in your kitchen. Ask your friends for ideas. Then put it all together in a book and self-publish fifty copies. Get the word out through your neighbors and see how fast they fly off your shelves.

☠ $ *tried it* ○

951 **OFFER COOKING LESSONS.** Turn your kitchen into a classroom. Print up a nicely worded syllabus with, say, ten lessons—everything from soups to sautéing. Put fliers up around the neighborhood, especially in any local cookware shops. And at the end of the course, have the students cook a dinner for you and your family.

☠ $ $ *tried it* ○

952 **BECOME A PERSONAL CHEF.** Lots of busy people don't have time to cook for themselves, but they've got the money to hire someone to do it for them. Advertise your services. Be sure to include some recommendations from friends and acquaintances who've enjoyed your cooking.

☠ ☠ $ $ $ *tried it* ○

953 **CATER ROMANTIC DINNERS FOR TWO.** Filet mignon. Fresh asparagus with a creamy hollandaise sauce. A fine red wine, and candlelight. You can take care of all the details, and your clients can keep their minds on romance. Just be sure to make yourself scarce as soon as dinner is served and the candles are burning low.

☠ $ $ *tried it* ○

954 **GET PAID FOR FLAVORING POPCORN.** Companies like Dale & Thomas have made small fortunes providing corn connoisseurs with tasty alternatives to Jiffy Pop. Put your palette to good use and create flavor combinations that are out of this world. Package the popped corn in decorative tins and sell them online or at local fairs.

☠ $ $ *tried it* ○

955 **MAKE YOUR OWN CHEESE.** It's not just for the French anymore. You too can create smelly, delicious cheese in your own home, and then sell it to cheese snobs. Check out recipes for various varieties on GourmetSleuth.com. Be careful though—a couple miscued steps and you could turn your money-making scheme into a stink bomb that destroys your house.

☠ ☠ ☠ $ $ *tried it* ○

956 **MARKET YOUR OWN MACROBIOTIC MEALS.** A recent trend with fad-dieters is to follow suit with Gwyneth Paltrow and go macrobiotic. Unfortunately for them, this grain-heavy dietary regiment isn't the easiest thing to prepare. Fortunately for you, these types of dieters will pay anything to follow the weight-loss advice of their favorite stars. If you have a handle on making macrobiotic meals, cook them up in bulk and individually package them. Then sell them to your local macrobioticians.

☠ ☠ $ $ $ *tried it* ○

957 **WORK AS A FOR-HIRE SUSHI CHEF.** There are a few types of food that are definitely harder to create on your own than others. Sushi is certainly one of them. However, if you know how to slice and wrap sushi with your own set of hocho and makisu then maybe you have what it takes to be an at-home sushi chef—charging top dollar for *very* fresh meals.

☠ ☠ $ $ $ *tried it* ○

Cook Up Some Cash

958 **SELL COOKIE DOUGH.** Make up a ton of raw cookie dough. Put it in airtight plastic bags with attractive labels, cooking instructions, and maybe a few ribbons to brighten it up. Set up a table at the next school event and post fliers in the local supermarket. People will flock to get your homemade cookies they can bake in their own ovens.

☠ $ *tried it* ○

959 **PACKAGE YOUR OWN CAKE MIX.** It's simple. Put together the dry ingredient for your favorite cake in a bag with a label. Tell the buyer how many eggs and how much water to add and how long to bake and what temperature. If you want, give it a cute name: Auntie Sallie's Down Home Sinfully Delicious Cakes.

☠ $ *tried it* ○

960 **HOST A BAKE SALE.** They're not just for church fundraisers anymore! If you're a whiz with a whisk, cash in on your talent by selling your treats for profit. Sure, it's a little juvenile, but any venture that involves frosting seems like a no-brainer.

☠ $ *tried it* ○

961 **MAKE AND SELL DELI SANDWICHES.** Try this at a fair or a football or baseball game. Stock up on bologna, mozzarella, pepperoni, lettuce, and plenty of other ingredients. Have four or five different kinds of bread. Slather on the mayonnaise or mustard and listen for the happy customers.

☠ $ *tried it* ○

Cook Up Some Cash

962 **SELL YOUR OWN BBQ SAUCE.** It's the one you've been perfecting for the past five summers. Adding a little dry mustard here. A little more hot sauce there. A few ounces of beer and a couple of tablespoonfuls of whiskey. Now you're ready to try it out on the world. Save old bottles, wash them clean and disinfect them, and make up some cute labels to paste on.

☠   *$*   *tried it* ○

963 **BOTTLE YOUR OWN JUICE.** Buy fruits and vegetables in bulk—which means, buy them *fresh*. Invest in a good industrial-strength juicer, and collect lots of bottles in which to sell the juices you make. Try some blends; tomato-basil or plum-apricot might work.

☠   *$ $*   *tried it* ○

964 **SELL PROTEIN SHAKES.** Everyone's got a health shake that makes them feel great. What's yours? Start mixing and find out. Once you've got it down, package it, label it, and put it up for sale. Your local health food store and gym are great places to advertise.

☠   *$*   *tried it* ○

965 **SELL CUPCAKES AT WORK.** Take a cake decorating class or buy a book about it. Then, after some experimenting at home (your family will be happy to eat the experiments!), bring gourmet cupcakes into work. If people like them, you may be asked to make some for parties.

☠   *$*   *tried it* ○

966 **SELL PIZZA SLICES LATE AT NIGHT.** Sometimes people don't want a whole pizza—just a slice is great. This can work really well if you live near a college campus where students are pulling all-nighters. Make up a bunch of pizzas, slice 'em, and get ready to jump in your car when the phone rings with a hungry customer.

☠ $ *tried it* ○

967 **SELL FOOD OUTSIDE A BAR.** After a long night's boozing, nothing tastes better than poutain smothered in gravy and cheese. Don't know what poutain is? Suffice it to say that the drunker you are, the tastier it is. Make sure you have all the necessary permits before you start ladling it out.

☠ $ $ *tried it* ○

968 **SELL FOOD IN A CONCERT LOT.** Drunk people are always hungry. So are people who've just been dancing for three hours. Whether it's pizza, tacos, or French fries, whip up a batch and hawk them to concert-goers on their way out. Make sure to check local ordinances for legality issues.

☠ $ $ *tried it* ○

969 **SELL COFFEE TO PICKETERS.** In times of industrial unrest, union picketers are hitting the streets, often early in the morning. Set up a small stand to serve coffee and donuts and clean up. Who knows? They may even make you an honorary union member.

☠ $ *tried it* ○

970 **SELL HOMEGROWN FRUIT.** Plant some apple trees, a peach tree, some raspberry, blueberry, and strawberry bushes. You can set up a stand at the local farmer's market. And the more trees and shrubs you plant, the less grass you'll have to mow in the summer!

☠️ $ $ *tried it* ○

971 **SELL HOMEGROWN VEGETABLES.** If you can plant big vegetable beds that produce a lot of produce, you may be able to strike a deal with some area restaurants to supply them with fresh veggies. Of course, this sort of thing takes quite a bit of maintenance, so get ready to do weeding, spraying, and pruning over the summer.

☠️ $ $ *tried it* ○

972 **SELL PIES.** A homemade pie is worth a lot to some people. The smell brings back memories of trips to grandmother's house and the holidays. Break out the pie plates and your favorite recipe and get cookin'! Peddle your pies to your neighbors and friends.

☠️ $ $ *tried it* ○

973 **COOK HOLIDAY DINNERS.** Not everyone sees the joy in cooking for three days before Thanksgiving or Christmas. Most people eat the same thing for the holidays so cook extras and pack them up to sell. You can freeze everything and send it along in a cooler.

☠️ ☠️ $ $ $ *tried it* ○

974 **GROW AND SELL HERBS.** All legal herbs of course, unless you happen to have a medical marijuana license, but that's a different entry. Grow the most popular herbs, like parsley, basil, oregano, and chives. You can set up a stand in the front of your house or bring them to a farmer's market.

☠️ $ *tried it* ○

975 **SELL PRODUCTS WITH ORGANIC EGGS.** Organic eggs from the market can run up to $4 a dozen! Jump on the organic trend train and start cooking up culinary creations that utilized these organic, unfertilized embryos. Check out entry 691 if you'd prefer to harvest the eggs yourself.

☠ ☠ $ *tried it* ○

976 **SELL YOUR OWN SALSA.** If David "Big Papi" Ortiz can have his mug on a jar of salsa, don't think twice about selling your own. Sure, he's a famous ball player, but you've actually lovingly made the salsa with your own two hands. Think about baking your own tortilla chips to go with it.

☠ $ *tried it* ○

977 **SELL YOUR OWN GUACAMOLE.** A few avocadoes, some tomatoes, onions, and garlic and you have the core ingredients of a great guac. Really good guacamole is hard to come by, so if you have a killer recipe, use it to your advantage. You can serve it at your next party, then when everyone says they love it, ask if they'd want to buy a jar . . . or two.

☠ $ *tried it* ○

978 **MAKE YOUR OWN MAPLE SYRUP.** First off, you need to live in an area that has easy access to maple trees. If you do, purchase a tap at your local hardware store and start draining the delicious goo into buckets. The boiling and processing takes some work and skill, but if you have the equipment and are a quick learner, you can start selling little jugs of your own.

☠ ☠ ☠ $ $ *tried it* ○

979 **SELL HOMEMADE ICE CREAM.** If you have an ice cream machine stuck in the closet somewhere, you're sitting on a goldmine. Remember the utter excitement you felt hearing the music of the ice cream truck in the summer? Little kids will be clamoring for some of your ice cream. A pack of cones, some sprinkles and you are in business.

☠ ☠ $ *tried it* ○

980 **SELL HOMEMADE CHOCOLATE.** Chocolate is a classic gift on Valentine's Day. Make your own truffles and kisses and sell them to those poor saps looking for a last minute gift for their girl. If they get lucky, you might too . . with a big tip and another order.

☠ $ *tried it* ○

981 **SELL FUDGE.** Everyone loves ooey gooey fudge. Make a couple trays of peanut butter, penuche, and double chocolate fudge and sell it at a bake sale or a fundraiser. It's sure to be a hit.

☠ $ *tried it* ○

982 **SELL HERBAL REMEDIES.** Whether it's a lemon herb lip balm or a tonic to fill in your bald spot, herbal remedies are popular. People like to use all natural items when they can, and with everyone going organic, now's the time to sell your own herbal remedies. Make sure you find out if they have allergies before you sell anything to them.

☠ ☠ ☠ $ $ *tried it* ○

983 **MAKE AND SELL ICED TEA.** Think of it as a lemonade stand but classier. Homemade iced tea is fantastic on a hot summer day, and you can make more than one flavor to please a variety of customers.

☠ $ *tried it* ○

984 **GRIND SPICES.** Ground spices can cost a pretty penny, and no one wants to pay $8 for a small jar of cinnamon. If you have a mortar and pestle or one of those small, handy coffee grinders you can grind your own.

☠   **$**   *tried it* ○

985 **GIVE BAKING LESSONS.** If you can bake a cake, a pie, cupcakes, and cookies, you can teach others. People will love to learn how they can make a SpongeBob SquarePants cake for their four-year-old. If you have the skill, charge a little bit extra and teach a "specialty cake" class.

☠ ☠   **$ $**   *tried it* ○

986 **BAKE BREAD.** Make dough to make dough. There was a reason Grandma Louisa gave you her top-secret recipe for her world-famous cherry-almond bread. Watch out, Betty Crocker! (Just make sure you adhere to the necessary rules if you start a commercial operation.)

☠   **$**   *tried it* ○

987 **JAR ORGANIC BABY FOOD.** You can bet that yummy mummy down the street is worried sick about the unpronounceable ingredients in the jars of mashed bananas she buys. Just make sure you know what you're doing; food safety is no joke, especially when infants are involved.

☠ ☠   **$**   *tried it* ○

988 **SELL BIRTHDAY CAKES.** If little Timmy down the street wants an Elmo cake, say no problem, buddy. One Elmo cake on the way. A homemade cake is more personal and usually tastes better than the generic store-bought cake with the two-inch layer of butter cream frosting. If your customer wants an organic or gluten-free cake, try to accommodate and charge a little bit extra.

☠   **$ $**   *tried it* ○

989 **SELL WEDDING CAKES.** Nobody wants to promise their first born for a decent wedding cake. If you have some baking skills, offer to work with the bride and groom to make the cake of their dreams. Take pictures of your final product and build a portfolio.

☠ ☠ ☠　　　$ $　　　*tried it* ○

990 **SELL EROTIC BAKED GOODS.** If you can make a cake shaped like a penis or boobs, you can make money. Get creative with the frosting job and you'll have bachelorette party attendees everywhere squealing with joy. For these treats you can go as wild as you want. So get out the flour and go to your dirty place.

☠ ☠ ☠　　　$ $　　　*tried it* ○

991 **HIRE OUT AS A PERSONAL NUTRITIONIST.** If you see your friends and family members eating crap all day and you know how to fix it, offer to be their personal nutritionist. Go to their house and clean out their cupboards and fridge, then take them shopping. Professional nutritionists make bank, but charge what you think is right.

☠ ☠　　　$ $　　　*tried it* ○

992 **SELL TRAIL MIX.** Set up a stand near your local hiking trails and sell bags of your mix to those hungry hikers. Put together some peanuts, chocolate-covered candies, rice cereal squares, and raisins. Make a few different kinds to target the health nuts and their kids.

☠　　　$　　　*tried it* ○

Cook Up Some Cash

993 **MAKE AND SELL GRANOLA.** Granola is a super-simple way to dress up yogurt or great on its own. It's so easy to make, so why do they charge so much for it in the stores? Offer a lot of flavors and varieties and you'll have customers for life.

☠ $ *tried it* ○

994 **SELL HEALTH FOOD SNACKS.** Make some tasty protein bars or shakes and stand outside your gym and wait for starving chicks to come out of Pilates. If you get some positive feedback, ask the owner of your gym if she would display them. Give out free samples and build your fan base.

☠ $ $ *tried it* ○

995 **MAKE JERKY.** Jerky has been around forever. A favorite treat for Native Americans, it's proven itself useful while traveling long distances to hunt for buffalo or just for a road trip. A food dehydrator will make this task a lot easier, but if you don't have one, you can use the oven.

☠ ☠ $ $ *tried it* ○

996 **MAKE AND SELL ROCK CANDY.** Remember when you would almost break your teeth on the sugar crystals but you didn't care because it tasted so good? Who thought sugar on a stick would be such a hit. Check out *www.science bob.com/experiments/rockcandy.php* for a great recipe.

☠ $ *tried it* ○

997 **MAKE AND SELL YOUR OWN PASTA.** Flour. Eggs. Water. Start-up costs don't get any lower than that. Get your friends and neighbors hooked and see what happens when you debut your chipotle-infused fettuccine. (Note that you'll need to abide by food safety rules and regulations if you take your business commercial.)

☠ $ *tried it* ○

998 **FLAVOR AND BOTTLE OIL.** Olive oil is boring—no matter how extra virgin it is. These days, infused oils are all the rage. Snip some herbs and let them set in a fancy bottle with some olive oil. Or maybe kick it up a notch with some spicy peppers. The flavor combinations are endless.

☠ $ $ *tried it* ○

999 **MARKET YOUR OWN DIPPING POWDER.** Restaurants will often accompany their basket of bread with a plate of spices and cheese that the server pours oil over once you sit. Create and bottle your own addictive dipping powder that people can serve in their own homes. Pair it up with your own special oil and double your profits.

☠ $ $ *tried it* ○

1000 **SELL SEA SALT.** This is actually easier than it seems. Just fill up a bathlike container with seawater and leave it outside in the sun to evaporate. What you have left are a bunch of crystals at the bottom, and that's salt. Bottle it up, tie a ribbon around it, and presto. Delicious sea salt, and your customers don't have to pay an arm and a leg for it.

☠ $ $ *tried it* ○

1001 **BOTTLE YOUR OWN SODA.** You can buy machines to make your own soda at *www.sodaclubusa.com/prodinfo.htm*. If you find some antique bottles, you can use them to bottle your soda. People will love the kitschy, old-time feel of the bottles and think they are getting a real deal.

☠ ☠ $ *tried it* ○

Resources

Following is a list of online resources that will help you in your quest to master the side hustle.

About.com

www.about.com

Not exactly sure how to pull one of these entries off? Search this site for some instructional advice.

AirBed & Breakfast

www.airbedandbreakfast.com

Allows you to rent your couch or an airbed to travelers looking to stay overnight on the cheap.

Amazon.com

www.amazon.com

An online retailer that allows for plenty of reselling opportunities, whether you have books, movies, or CDs to sell.

CafePress

www.cafepress.com

Set up shop on this site that lets you upload and sell designs for everything from t-shirts to coffee mugs.

Cash Crate

www.cashcrate.com

This site organizes all types of online offers in one place.

ClinicalTrials.gov

http://clinicaltrials.gov

A service of the United States National Institute of Health, it provides listings of clinical trials throughout the country.

Consumer Search

www.consumersearch.com

Will provide compensation for your critiques of a wide variety of products.

Craftster

www.craftster.com

Connect with fellow crafters and sell what you've made on this community site.

DIY Network

www.diynetwork.com

Get tips on how to get your hands dirty from this informative site.

DVD Pawn

www.dvdpawn.com

A secure site that buys your unwanted DVDs, which cuts out having to wait for an interested party to contact you from an auction or resale site.

Resources

e-Focus Groups

www.e-focusgroups.com

The place to get your e-pinion on—and get paid for it; sign up to be considered for their next focus group panel.

eBay

www.ebay.com

It's the most popular online auction site; you can post just about anything you're willing to part with.

Etsy

www.etsy.com

A great place to sell all sorts of crafts that you create.

Facebook

www.facebook.com

You can sell items on the Facebook marketplace, or use it as a tool to market your product or service.

Festival Network Online

www.festivalnet.com

Find when and where the next local craft fair is taking place so you can hock your wares in person.

Filming Locations, LLC

www.filminglocations.com

Searches for the next best place to film a movie for various studios; submit pictures of your home for consideration on the site.

FreelanceWriting.com

www.freelancewriting.com

Find freelance writing gigs on this site, as well as postings about writing contests.

Games : : Tester

www.gamestester.com

It's an online job board for people who think they can hack it in the video game industry.

The Hair Trader

www.thehairtrader.com

Post a picture of the long locks you're willing to part with and see if anyone will purchase them.

Major League Gaming

www.mlgpro.com

Check out this site to sign up for the next gaming tournament.

MediaBistro.com

www.mediabistro.com

Use this site to either post your resume for media-related freelance work, or search job postings for a gig.

Monster.com

www.monster.com

A premiere job search site, it allows you to find part-time employment as well as post your resume for consideration for freelance work.

Resources

Publishers Marketplace

www.publishersmarketplace.com

Post a synopsis of your book online and see if any editors or agents are interested.

RanchWork.com

www.ranchwork.com

Visit this site that specializes in job listings for people who want to make it out on the range.

Recycle In Me

www.recycleinme.com

A website that lists locations of scrap yards in your area, which will purchase any scrap metal you collect; the site also has "Wanted" ads looking for specific types of scrap metal and equipment.

The U.S. Government's Official Web Portal

www.usa.gov

It's best to make sure what you're about to do to earn some cash is actually legal in your area, and you do not need to secure any permits or licenses before you start.

Universal Class

www.universalclass.com

Interested in one of the entries, but have no idea how to pull it off? Sign up for a class online.

Vista Print

www.vistaprint.com

It's a one-stop shop for all of your promotional needs if you plan on making money by launching a side business.

Voices.com

www.voices.com

Collects job listings for voiceover work all in one place; it also allows you to post an audio resume.

Weblogs, Inc.

www.weblogsinc.com

Your jumping-off point to get paid for blogging.

WordPress.com

www.wordpress.com

The perfect jumping-off point if you want to try and make big bucks off your online writing.

Writer's Digest

www.writersdigest.com

Has an extensive collection of writing competitions you can enter.

Resources

Acknowledgments

Thanks go to everyone at Adams Media for helping to make a project like this possible, with special thanks to Erin Alexander, Stephanie Bernardo, Karen Cooper, Colleen Cunningham, Casey Ebert, Matt LeBlanc, and Paula Munier.

We would like to acknowledge the work done by the contributors to this book, without whom you'd be buying a bunch of blank pages. They are:

Peter Archer
Katie Corcoran Lytle
Matt Glazer
Elizabeth Kassab
Andrea Norville
Meredith O'Hayre
Brendan O'Neill
Katrina Schroeder

And to Trent Hamm for lending his sharp financial eye and love of the "side hustle."